Soccer Coach's Guide to Practices, Drills & Skill Training

BUTCH LAUFFER &
SANDY DAVIE

Sterling Publishing Co., Inc.   New York

DEDICATIONS

To my wife, Bertha, and my son, Blake, for their continual understanding. Also to all of my friends who help keep this game fun.

—Butch Lauffer

To my wife, Sue, for her love, encouragement, and understanding. To my three sons, Alan, Stuart, and Craig. To the fond memories of William Norrie who quietly encouraged me and of my grandfather, George Davie, who introduced me to *The Beautiful Game*. And to the countless people who have influenced my playing and coaching career, thank you.

—Sandy Davie

ACKNOWLEDGMENTS

Suzanne Davie—Editing/Typing, Ft. Myers, Florida

Linda Kay—Photographs, Ft. Worth, Texas

Paula Wells—Illustrations, Kingwood, Texas

Eric Davis—Fitness Consultant, Ft. Worth, Texas

Peter Moore—Equipment, President Patrick U.S.A.

Players—Texas Longhorns, Dallas, Texas

    Ft. Worth United, Ft. Worth, Texas

    Texas Christian University, Ft. Worth, Texas

    Spring/Lone Stars Soccer Club, Spring, Texas

10 9 8 7 6 5 4 3 2

First paperback edition published in 1992 by
Sterling Publishing Company, Inc.
387 Park Avenue South, New York, N.Y. 10016
© 1991 by Butch Lauffer & Sandy Davie
Distributed in Canada by Sterling Publishing
% Canadian Manda Group, P.O. Box 920, Station U
Toronto, Ontario, Canada M8Z 5P9
Distributed in Great Britain and Europe by Cassell PLC
Villiers House, 41/47 Strand, London WC2N 5JE, England
Distributed in Australia by Capricorn Link Ltd.
P.O. Box 665, Lane Cove, NSW 2066
Manufactured in the United States of America
All rights reserved

Sterling ISBN 0-8069-8218-7 Trade
      0-8069-8219-5 Paper

Edited by Rodman Neumann

Library of Congress Cataloging-in-Publication Data

Lauffer, Robert.
  Soccer coach's guide to practices, drills & skill training / by Butch Lauffer & Sandy Davie.
    p. cm.
  Includes index.
  ISBN 0-8069-8218-7
  1. Soccer—Coaching. 2. Soccer—Training. I. Davie, Sandy. II. Title. III. Title: Soccer coach's guide to practices, drills, and skill training.
GV943.8.L39 1991
796.334'07'7 dc20
                                     91-19117
                                     CIP

Contents

Introduction 5

I. Basic Principles & Techniques 7
The Coach's Reference 7
  Dribbling 7
  Shielding 10
  Passing 12
  Push Pass 13
  Swerve Pass 14
  Instep Drive 16
  Kicking with the Outside of the Foot 17
  Lofted Pass 18
  Chipping 19
  Full Volleys 20
  Ground & Aerial Control 27
  Tackling 36
  Heading 36
  Goalkeeping 39

II. Injury Management 43
  Stretching 43
  Fluids 45
  Heat Illnesses 45
  Shin Splints 45
  Flesh Wounds 45

III. U-8 Drills & Practices: (under age 8) 47
Practices 48
  Warm-up 48
  Dribbling 49
  Passing 51
  Instep Drive 55
  Control 57
  Heading 60
  Goalkeeping 62
Team Games 66

IV. U-10 Drills & Practices: (under age 10)   69
   Practices   70
      Warm-up   70
      Shielding   70
      Moves—Turns   72
      Kicking   74
      Control   80
      Heading   85
      Tackling   86
      Goalkeeping   88
   Team Games   94

V. U-12 Drills & Practices: (under age 12)   103
   Practices   104
      Warm-up   104
      Dribbling   105
      Kicking   108
      Control   115
      Heading   119
      Goalkeeping   121
   Team Games   130

VI. U-15 Drills & Practices (under age 15)   132
   Practices   133
      Warm-up   133
      Dribbling   134
      Kicking   136
      Passing   138
      Aerial Control   146
      Heading   148
      Goalkeeping   149
   Team Games   155

About the Authors   158

Index   160

INTRODUCTION

Soccer is already the most popular game world-wide; but as its popularity continues to increase rapidly on the local level, we are faced with the increased need for more parent and volunteer coaches. Based on our combined experience, we feel that greater thought must be given to the process by which we coach our young players.

COACHES' NEEDS

Sensing the need for resources during our soccer travels across the country, we conceived of this guide. While conducting coaching courses, summer camps, and simply speaking with parent coaches, we developed the idea of this book to assist in teaching team coaches how to improve players' basic techniques and then perfect them through proper practice.

PLAYERS' PERFORMANCE

Of concern to us was the instances of young players dropping out of the sport. Our analysis indicates that the most common factors why youngsters drop out of sport are an overemphasis on winning, peer pressure, parent pressure, and not enough fun and enjoyment. In addition to helping the coach develop skills and techniques, the object of this guide is to encourage the player's sense of enjoyment.

We have identified two things which significantly impact the player's performance: coaching and competition. Overcoaching or too much competition at an inappropriate time in the player's development could, and indeed often does, lead to failure and disillusionment with the game. This leads some to eventually abandon the sport altogether.

LEARNING, MASTERY & ENCOURAGEMENT

We have designed this guide to serve the coach in several ways. The first and second chapters are basic reference material on skills and techniques from dribbling to goalkeeping on the one hand, and injury prevention and management on the other. Arguably soccer has the greatest range of techniques to be learned of any game in the world. Therefore, if these techniques are to be mastered, the coach and the players must invest sufficient time in the learning process.

To facilitate this learning process, the subsequent four chapters represent a tool for the coach in choosing, planning, and creating a practice strategy that will accomplish the goals of technique mastery and team development while encouraging the players' sense of fun and enjoyment. These four chapters covering the four young age groups—U-8 (under age 8), U-10, U-12, U-15—outline player and goalkeeping practices along with team games. Each of these practices can be expanded upon as the players progress. The coach is encouraged to think of new ways to adapt the exercises and to use them as inspiration for designing original practices suited to a particular need.

For our part we offer this resource and ask that you remember always the need for maximum player–ball contact. Consequently the practice should always feature the soccer ball—or indeed, soccer balls—prominently. And lastly, we remind you that the most effective practice is one that is well organized, safe, and enjoyable so that the players learn and remember what has been taught—thus returning and staying with the sport for many enjoyable years.

Robert "Butch" Lauffer
Alexander "Sandy" Davie

I

BASIC PRINCIPLES & TECHNIQUES

Here we provide a step-by-step explanation of each skill and technique including more than one hundred photos, the indentification of qualities and methods needed for proper execution, and lists of common faults to watch out for.

THE COACH'S REFERENCE

The coach will find that the appropriate chapter for the age group—U–8 (under age 8), U–10, U–12, U–15—will serve as the main resource for choosing, planning, and creating practical drill and practice exercises. Each of these "Drills & Practices" chapters is structured alike with progressive concentration on various techniques and skill developments followed by emphasis on principles of play and team games.

This first chapter is an encyclopedia of the basic principles, techniques, and skills that will be exercised and called on again and again during practice sessions and games.

DRIBBLING

Dribbling is the ability of a player to move the ball at a reasonable pace, keeping it close to the feet under pressure from an opponent. Dribbling is one of the most exciting parts of the game of soccer: in a one-on-one or a one-on-two confrontation. A player with good dribbling skills can destroy the best organized defenses in the world. An example of this was Diego Maradonna's second goal for Argentina against England in the 1986 World Cup held in Mexico.

Dribbling is a player's way of self-expression during a game. As the game has matured with sophisticated defensive systems of play, we feel that as coaches, we should develop players who have the mentality, technical ability, and bravery to dribble and take opponents on. As coaches we should provide the environment for players to develop this technique so they can learn to handle success and failure. After the player has developed a wide range of feints, the coach and player must develop an understanding of when and where to dribble, in what parts of the field, and where to take risks.

Almost all exciting players are good dribblers of the ball, but there are high risks of losing possession. Restrict dribbling in the *defending* and *middle third* of the field (1.1) to make space for a clearing pass forward.

The foot surfaces which a good dribbler uses are the outside and the inside of the foot (1.2 and 1.3). Keep the ball close while scanning the field in between soft touches using the inside and outside of each foot just below the middle of the ball.

The Inside of the foot allows the player to push or carry the ball.

The Outside of the foot is used when the player is running at speed.

The Sole of the foot is used to stop the ball or pull it back to change direction.

Dribbling is a means to an end, not an end in itself. The objective is to score, not merely dribble.

Develop Dribbling in the Attacking Third

- **Create Pressure.** Running at opponents.

- **Penetration.** Getting behind opponents.

- **Space for Shooting.** Deceiving opponents by faking to create space between defending players for a shot.

1.1

Qualities of Effective Dribbling

- **Head up—Awareness.** Scan the field in between touches. Look at the ball through the bottom half of your eyes. Be aware of team-mates and opponents as well as the opening and closing of spaces.

- **Close Control.** A player should use either foot keeping the ball within a stride and be able to change direction quickly without losing the ball to an opponent.

- **Bent Knees—Balance.** A low center of gravity; knees must be bent to allow the player to stop, start, accelerate, and change direction.

- **Change of Direction.** The players ability to beat opponents by quick–sharp changes of direction and cutbacks.

- **Change of Pace.** The players ability to use a change of tempo to get past opponents.

- **Feints.** Use of the body to get the opponent off balance while manipulating the ball with both feet.

- **Bravery.** Players must be brave enough to attempt to get past opponents in and around the penalty box, knowing they will probably be kicked or fouled. This mentality will provide great dividends in the form of goals, penalty kicks, and free kicks.

Common Faults

- Head down.
- Dribbling with the toe.
- Ball too far away.
- Attempting to beat the same opponent twice.
- Upright stance.
- No change of pace or direction.

1.2

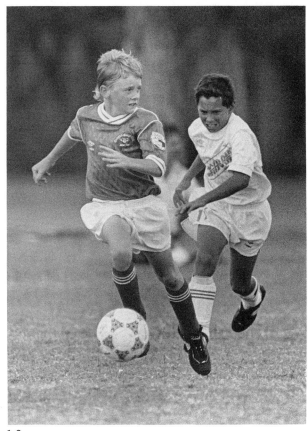

1.3

SHIELDING

When shielding the soccer ball the attacking player should be positioned sideways-on, towards the opponent. The attacker should then form a long barrier by bending the knee and extending the arm closest to the opponent. The other arm should be out for balance and the ball on the attacker's farthest foot (1.4). Being sideways-on also enables the attacking player to have vision which will increase the chance of turning.

A common fault is that, when an attacking player shields the ball flat-on, the attacker will not be able to make a long barrier. This makes it easier for an opponent to poke the ball away (1.5). This will cut down on the attacker's vision and hinder the ability to turn quickly.

If an opponent challenges from behind, the attacker can then go towards the space that the opponent has left (1.6, 1.7). The attacker can also pivot, change feet and stay sideways onto the opponent (1.8, 1.9, 1.10).

1.5

1.4

1.6

1.7

1.10

1.8

1.9

11

If an opponent challenges across the face of the attacker, the attacker can pivot and turn away from the opponent (1.11, 1.12), using the inside of the farthest foot to pull the ball from behind and go forward.

Because of the number of attacking front players, it is often necessary that they have the ability to shield the ball well (1.13). This will then create time to allow supporting players to get forward.

Irrespective of the foot surface being used, the qualities of a good pass are:

- **Accuracy.** Playing to feet or in front of a teammate.

- **Weight.** Not too hard, not too soft.

- **Timing.** Release the pass.

- **Disguise.** Concealing your intention from opponents.

1.11

1.12

Common Faults

- Coming to the ball flat-on.
- Not holding the ball with the farthest foot.
- Receiving the ball with the inside of the foot.
- Not making a long barrier.
- Lack of vision.

1.13

PUSH PASS

Inside of the Foot Kicking

The push pass (kicking the soccer ball with the inside of the foot) is the most accurate method of kicking. It is also the easiest kicking method that a soccer player will learn. The push pass provides the largest surface a soccer player uses in kicking. The part of the foot used should be from the bottom of the big toe joint area to the bottom half of the arch of the foot. The approach of the player to the ball should be in a straight line (1.14). The non-kicking foot should be slightly behind the ball and pointing at the intended target (1.15).

1.15

1.14

The kicking foot should be pointed outward at a right angle with the toe pointing upwards. The foot should be three to five inches off the ground so that the player can strike the ball at the midline or slightly above the midline, enabling the ball to stay on the ground (1.16). Again, the height of the foot will vary depending on the age of the player and the ball size used (3-4-5). The knee should be bent and the swing action from the hip followed by a proper follow-through, ending up pointing at the intended target (1.17).

1.16

1.17

The arms are used for balance (1.18). If the player is right-footed, the right arm should be almost straight out from the body. The left arm should be swung out as the kicking leg backswing is in motion, and, as it comes forward, the left arm comes back in and across the kicker's chest.

1.19

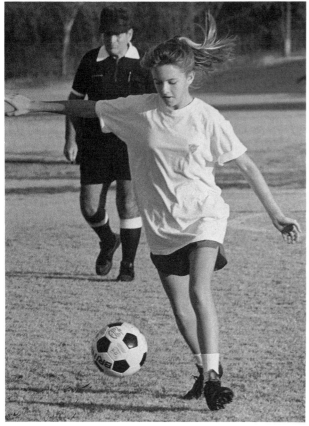
1.18

Common faults with very young players are that they will approach the ball from the side and attempt to use the inside of the foot, therefore making it mechanically impossible to pass the ball accurately (1.19).

Other common faults with young players are that when approaching the ball correctly—which is in a straight line—they may swing across their own body, again making it impossible to kick the ball accurately.

Or they do not open the foot to a right angle and kick the ball on the side, therefore the spin of the ball will be from left to right, or right to left, when it should have topspin.

SWERVE PASS

Inside of the Foot

When swerving a pass using the inside of the foot the approach should be towards the target at an angle not exceeding 45 degrees (1.20).

The nonkicking foot should be approximately 10–12 inches to the side of the ball with the leg slightly bent at the knee. The upper body should be inclined forward slightly, and balance maintained by the arms.

The eyes should be fixed off-center, on the ball, where contact is to be made. The backswing of the kicking leg should start simultaneously when taking the final step of the approach (1.21). The leg should be whipped forwards from the hip; on impact the knee should be slightly bent and the joints held tight (1.22). A low pass or shot will require that contact be made with the ball, off-center, through the midline or above.

For a higher trajectory the upper part of the body should lean slightly backwards and the ball struck, off-center and below the midline. The extent of the backwards lean will determine the height that the player wishes to achieve with the ball.

1.20

1.21

1.23

1.22

Following impact, the kicking leg should swing through from the hip (1.23). The backward lean of the upper body should be at its greatest after the follow-through and straightened as soon as the kicking foot returns to the ground.

Common Faults

- Failure to keep eyes on the ball.
- Wrong approach angle.
- The nonkicking foot too far away from the ball.
- Incorrect follow-through.

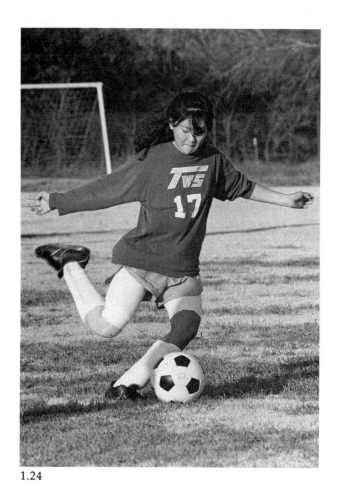

1.24

THE INSTEP DRIVE (LACES)

The instep drive is the most fluid method of striking a ball. The ball should be struck with the shoelace part of the foot, with the toe pointed down and the ankle locked (1.24). The approach to the ball should be from a slight angle allowing the player a full backswing (1.25). The nonkicking foot should be placed next to the ball and slightly behind it, as well as pointing towards the intended target. The kicking foot knee should be slightly bent during the backswing with the swing motion coming from the hip (1.26). When kicking this way the player will look up and identify the target, then look down when ready to strike the ball.

When shooting at goal, the player should try to land on the shooting foot that will allow a full transfer of body weight. The height of the kick will be determined by the player moving the body forward over the ball. The knee should be over the ball also. The more forward the body position is the lower the shot will be.

If the player is right-footed, then the right arm should be directly behind the players body for balance (1.27). The left arm starts out by coming across the chest and proceeds in a counterclockwise motion, ending up behind the body.

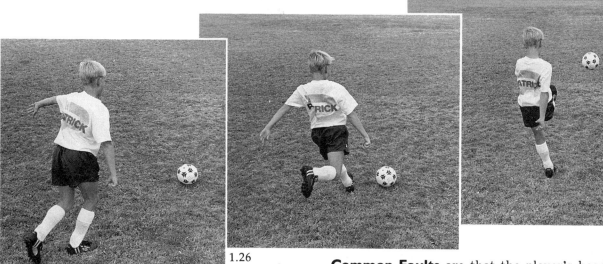

1.25

1.26

1.27

Common Faults are that the player's head will come up too soon making the player miskick and that the player's toe will come up too soon making the player toe-kick.

KICKING WITH THE OUTSIDE OF THE FOOT

When kicking the ball with the outside of the foot, if approached at an angle, it will go straight; if approached straight on, it will bend or swerve. This method can be used to perform one of three things:

- Bend the ball into the path of the teammate.
- Bend the ball away from the intended player into space to run onto.
- Bend the ball during a shot on goal.

When the ball is struck with the outside of the foot, the kicking foot should be pointed down and towards the inside of the player with the ankle locked (1.28). The foot should strike the ball off center which will make the ball bend (1.29).

The knee should be bent with the kicking action coming from the hip (1.30, 1.31). The follow-through should have the kicking leg come across the players body (1.32). The nonkicking foot should be 8–10 inches from the ball and slightly behind it.

If the player is kicking with the right foot then the right arm will stay to the side of the player for balance. The left arm will start out to the side and

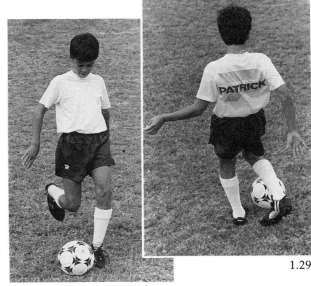

1.28

1.29

as the player moves forward to kick, the arm will come across the chest.

When shooting on goal, try and have the player end up on the shooting foot. The transfer of weight onto the front foot will increase the power in the shot. When performing this technique, it is important that the player keep the head down and the body over the ball.

1.30

1.31

1.32

Common Faults

- Approach angle wrong.
- Nonkicking foot too far away from the ball.
- The player unlocking the ankle.

LOFTED PASS

The lofted pass is a skill used in many aspects of the game of soccer. Goalkeepers use it when taking goal kicks. Defenders on occasion when clearing the ball out of a danger area. Attackers are required to use it when crossing the ball into the penalty box, and it is also required when taking corner kicks and free kicks.

1.33

1.34

The approach to the ball is at an angle so that the player has a full range of motion from the hip (1.33, 1.34). The arm action is the same as the instep drive. If the kicker is a right-footed player the right arm should be slightly behind and to the side of the body for balance (1.35); the left arm starts out coming across the chest proceeding in a counterclockwise motion, ending up perpendicular with the kicker's body (1.36).

The players body position should be leaning away and back from the ball, which provides lift. The nonkicking foot should be 8–10 inches to the side and slightly behind the ball.

The position of the toe of the kicking foot should be pointed away from the player, with the ankle locked. The instep of the foot should strike the ball through the bottom half, making it rise. The player should also hit through the middle of the ball to avoid pulling or slicing.

1.35

1.36

Common Faults

- No approach angle.
- Head comes up too early.
- Nonkicking foot too close or too far away.
- Kicking with the wrong foot surface.
- Ankle unlocked.

18

CHIPPING

When chipping the soccer ball, the approach angle should be straight on to the ball with the arms out for balance and protection (1.37). The body should be leaning over the ball and the player's head down and locked (1.38). Using a descending blow, the kicking action should be a sharp jab from the knee with very little or no follow-through (1.39). Point-of-contact should be the top of the toe area of the kicking foot, striking completely below the ball. This kicking action will provide a sharp vertical trajectory over a short distance.

1.37

1.38

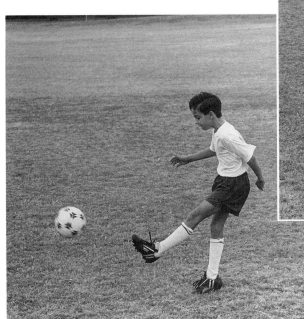

1.39

This particular type of skill can be used to get over and/or behind opponents when other passing alternatives are not available.

Common Faults

- Head raised too early.
- Failure to get under the ball.
- Kicking the ground.
- Toe punting.
- Using the whole leg.
- A long follow-through.

FULL VOLLEYS

A full volley is a kicking method where the player kicks the ball before it touches the ground. This technique can be performed in one of two ways: either by approaching down the line of flight of the ball or across the line of flight of the ball.

Striking at the Goal—Inside of the Foot Volley

The approach should be down the line of flight of the ball. The nonkicking foot should be pointing towards the intended target. The knee of the non-kicking leg should be slightly flexed to give balance and stability. The kicking action starts with the lifting and opening up of the kicking leg from the hip (1.40). The knee should be locked with the final kicking action coming from the knee down, where the lower leg is stiff. The contact foot should be at a right angle with the ankle locked (1.41). The foot strikes the ball at the midline or slightly above to keep it low. The follow-through should be short and towards the target.

The body should be upright and slightly leaning back. Arms are out and almost shoulder high for balance, composure, and protection. The head should be steady and the eyes fixed firmly on the ball.

Common Faults

- Head up.
- Leaning back.
- Getting too far under the ball.
- Swinging the kicking leg from the hip across the body.

1.41

1.40

Attacking—Instep Volley (Laces)

The approach should be down the line of flight of the ball. The nonkicking foot should be pointing towards the intended target. The knee of the non-kicking leg should be slightly flexed for balance and stability. The kicking action starts with the raising of the knee of the kicking foot (1.42). The final kicking action should be from the knee down

1.42

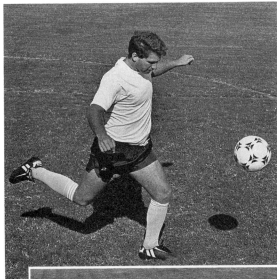
1.43

with the lower leg stiff. The toes of the contact foot should be pointing towards the ground with the ankle locked and the knee over the top of the ball (1.43).

The foot should make contact with the center of the ball on the lace part of the shoe at the midline or slightly above to keep the ball low. The body should be upright and slightly closed. Arms should be out and almost shoulder high; the head should be steady and the eyes firmly fixed on the ball.

Common Faults

- Head up.
- Failure to get knee over the ball.
- Leaning back.
- Kicking the ball off center.
- Failure to land on the shooting foot.
- Failure to keep the toe pointing down.

Attacking—Outside of the Foot Volley

The approach should be down the line of flight of the ball. The nonkicking foot should be pointing towards the intended target (1.44). The knee of the nonkicking leg should be slightly flexed to give balance and stability (1.45). The kicking action starts with the raising of the knee from the hip of the kicking foot (1.46). The knee should be brought across the thigh of the nonkicking leg and contact made from the area of the small toe to midway down the outside of the foot.

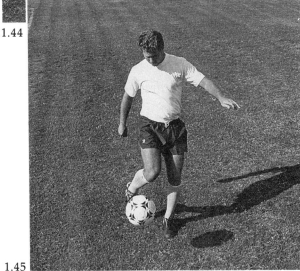
1.44

1.45

The toe of the kicking foot should be pointed down and inward towards the kicker. The attacker, depending on power needed, may land on the kicking foot. The body should be upright with the left

1.46

1.47

arm starting outward from the body and coming across the chest. The right arm should be out, hanging down for balance (1.47). The ball should be struck through left of center at the midline; if left-footed, the opposite will apply. By striking the ball off center, this will make the ball swerve.

Common Faults

- Head up.
- Leaning back.
- Contact too far to the side of the ball.
- Underestimating the speed of flight of the ball.

Defending—Full Volley

When players use the technique of a full volley for defending purposes, there are a few points to consider:

Coaching Points

- The defender must attack the ball.
- The defender should attempt to play the ball high (1.48). Height will give the defending team time to reorganize and mark opponents.

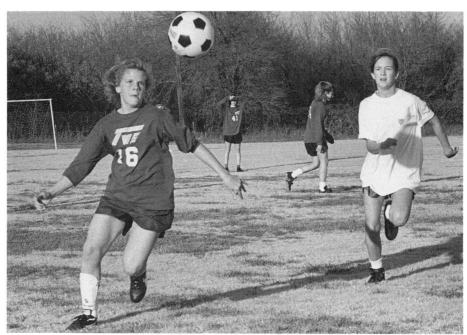

1.48

- Length—to remove the immediate danger at goal.
- Width—to take pressure off the goal by reducing the opponents target area; this could also provide an opportunity to counter-attack down the less populated flanks.

Defending—Inside of the Foot Volley

When defending, the technique of the inside of the foot volley has similarities to that of the attacking volley in that the approach should still be down the line of flight of the ball. The kicking action should be the same, with the main differences being that when the foot strikes the ball, it should be *underneath* the midline (1.49), with the player leaning well back to give it height (1.50).

1.49

1.50

Defending—Instep Volley

The two major differences of the instep volley when defending are:

- The knee should *not* be over the ball (1.51).
- The foot should make contact *below* the ball (1.52).

A combination of these two principles as well as the player leaning back will ensure that the ball goes either high or far (1.53).

Common Faults

- Taking the eyes off the ball.
- Failure to attack the ball.
- Mistiming the kick.
- Lack of height and distance in the volley.

1.51

1.52

1.53

Attacking—Inside of the Foot Volley—Across the Line

When shooting on goal with the inside of the foot the player's nonkicking foot must be pointing towards the target, not past it.

The initial foot position will allow the player to open up and face the ball down its line of flight. This body position will allow the correct kicking technique. The movement starts with the knee being raised until the inside of the foot becomes level with the middle of the ball (1.54).

The kicking action is initiated from the hip where the whole leg is brought across the player's body and flight of the ball (1.55). The lower leg should be stiff, ankle locked, and the toe pointed upward. The arms are up and out for balance, head steady and eyes looking at the ball.

With young players, have them concentrate on preparing to receive the ball early, then watch it hit and leave their foot.

Common Faults

- The nonkicking foot, not pointing at goal.
- Player taking their eyes off the ball.
- Leaning back.
- Striking underneath the ball.
- Ankle not locked.

1.54

1.55

Attacking—Instep Volley—Across the Line

Goals scored from full volleys attacking across the line of flight of the ball can be both exciting and spectacular. However, some of these chances can, and do go astray. The preparation of the player before contact is made with the ball is one of the most important parts of performing this technique.

The player's back should virtually be turned towards the goal that is being attacked, as the player plants and pivots on the foot nearest to the goal, pointing it towards the target (1.56). The leading shoulder should fall away to allow the kicking leg to swing smoothly, enabling the player to strike over and through the ball, keeping the shot low and on target (1.57). The player's ankle must be locked and the toe pointing away (1.58).

1.56

It is essential that the player's head be steady, keeping the eyes on the ball until contact is made. The player should follow-through and land on the shooting foot.

1.58

1.57

Common Faults

- Planting the nonkicking foot in front of or past the target.
- Taking eyes off the ball.
- Leaning back.
- Striking underneath the ball.
- Striking the ball square and not sideways-on to the target.

Defending—Inside of the Foot & Instep Volleys—Across the Line

When defending, the inside volley (1.59) and the instep volley (1.60) have similarities to that of the attacking techniques. The two major differences are:

- Leaning well back.
- Striking underneath the ball.

Adopting both these principles will ensure height and distance.

1.59

1.60

Common Faults

- Head up.
- Underestimating the flight of the ball.
- Ankle not locked.
- Failure to lean back.
- Striking too far over the ball.

Attacking—Half Volley

When does a half volley occur? It occurs when a player's reflexes are not quick enough to permit a strike on the ball before it hits the ground.

1.61

1.62

The main differences between the half volley and the full volley are that in the half volley the kicking foot strikes the ball as it contacts the ground. The half volley has a much lower and faster trajectory than the full volley, therefore, having the advantage of reaching the target faster.

Half volley shooting chances occur from bouncing or dropping balls, lofted forward passes, corners, free kicks, and rebounds from the goal area (1.61). In most cases the attacking player will come in and meet the ball down its line of flight (1.62). The player should make contact with the laces part of the shoe slightly above the midline of the ball with the ankle locked and the toe pointing down (1.63). The knee should be bent and over the ball with the body leaning forward; this will keep the shot low. The head is steady, eyes on the ball; arms are downward and slightly bent for balance and protection; the follow-through is a short punch-like action. The nonkicking foot should be alongside the ball and pointing towards the target. if it is behind the ball, the shot will go high.

Common Faults

- Leaning back.
- Eyes not on the ball.
- Mistiming the bounce of the ball.
- Stretching for the ball.
- Toe not pointing down.

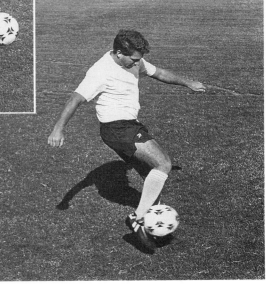

1.63

GROUND & AERIAL CONTROL

The definition of control in soccer is "a player's ability to bring a moving ball under control so that it can be shielded, dribbled, passed or shot." The player should keep eyes on the ball, select and move the controlling surface into its line of flight as early as possible, then relax and withdraw that surface on contact to produce a "cushion effect."

In today's game there is very rarely time to bring the ball to a complete standstill; therefore the ball should be taken into stride without stopping. The receiving player's concentration should be divided between the ball and the opposition; therefore when controlling the ball, the player's first touch is vitally important (1.64). Many times the first touch (or lack of first touch) may cause the player to:

- Lose possession of the ball.
- Miss scoring opportunities.
- Risk injury in attempting to regain possession.

The first touch will dictate the players next move.

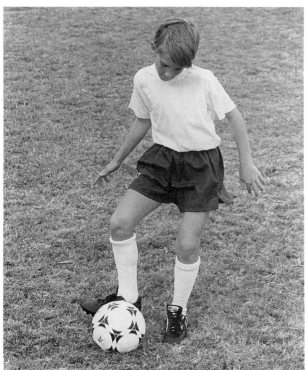

1.64

The most common parts of the body used to control the ball are:

- Inside of the foot.
- Outside of the foot.
- Instep.
- Sole of the foot.
- Thigh.
- Lower abdomen—when the ball bounces.
- Chest.
- Head.

Control becomes a skill when the player selects the correct controlling surface at the right tactical time.

Principles of Control

- Eyes on the ball.
- Select the controlling surface of the body as early as possible and move it into the line of flight of the ball.
- Relax the controlling surface on contact, or even withdraw it slightly.
- Control the ball for shielding, dribbling, passing, or shooting.
- Observe teammates, opponents, and the target area.

When controlling a dropping ball it is important that the player gets *underneath* it, and does not allow it to *bounce* as this will allow more time and space to make the best tactical decision or correct any error.

Young players can be guilty of allowing the ball one bounce before attempting to control. It is true that it is easier to control following the first bounce, however this will give an opponent time to close down space, pressure the controlling player, and possibly dispossess the player of the ball should the surface be uneven so that the ball is carried towards the opponent.

Note: When the basic principles of control are understood by young players, a progression towards moving situations in practice should be implemented to simulate game conditions.

Ground Control—Inside of the Foot

The surface most used to control a rolling ball along the ground is the inside of the foot.

At times a player will have to move forwards, backwards, or sideways to receive the ball. When a player receives a ball it has to be controlled cleanly; this will allow the player to shield, dribble, pass, or shoot.

With eyes fixed firmly on the ball, the nonkicking leg bent, and the arms out for balance, the player should relax and withdraw the inside of the controlling foot slightly to take the pace off the ball (1.64). Often joints held too tightly can cause the ball to rebound away from the player. The toe should be raised and the ankle locked with the controlling foot at a right angle. The leg should be turned outwards from the hip and the knee bent.

Common Faults

- Taking eyes off the ball.
- Not getting the controlling surface in line with the ball.
- Contact under the midline of the ball.
- Not withdrawing the controlling surface on contact.
- Contact with the wrong area of the foot.

It is important to remember that the controlling foot be raised so that it meets the ball at its midline or slightly above. This will keep the ball on the ground. If the controlling foot is not raised the ball will pop up in the air off the player's foot, therefore making it harder to control; a good defender will use this "air time" to advantage and curtail the attackers options (1.65).

Ground Control—Outside of the Foot

When controlling the ball with the outside of the foot, the player's nonkicking leg should be slightly flexed at the knee with the upper body leaning back (1.66). The arms should be down and away for balance and the eyes fixed firmly on the ball. The controlling leg should be bent as it moves to gather the ball with the controlling foot raised, and pointing inwards. If the ball is played too far away from the player's line of approach it may be necessary to have the controlling leg come all the way across the nonkicking leg.

Controlling with the outside of the foot can be used to a player's advantage as a setting up touch by playing the ball away from an opponent (1.67). This can create time and space in which to shoot, pass or dribble (1.68).

1.65

Ground Control & Turning—Inside of the Foot

When controlling and turning with the inside of the foot, the player should move towards the ball and position the nonkicking foot alongside it (1.69).

When the controlling foot meets the ball the player should pivot to the inside on the nonkicking foot (1.70). At the same time the controlling foot should be withdrawn, allowing the ball to roll through as the player performs a 180 degree turn (1.71).

1.66

1.67

1.68

1.69

1.70

1.71

Common Faults

- Failure to keep eyes on the ball.
- Not getting in line with the ball.
- Not turning the foot all the way in.
- Stiff joints—ball will bounce away.
- Contact below the midline of the ball will force the ball up in the air.

Another method is with the player approaching the ball *sideways-on*. This increases vision when checking away from an opponent. This type of control and turn is executed mainly by forwards attempting to create scoring opportunities against tight marking defenders (1.72).

The player should meet the ball and plant the nonkicking foot alongside it. The ball should roll and meet the controlling surface underneath the player (1.73, 1.74). Using the inside of the foot, the ball is guided behind the nonkicking leg while the player pivots on the nonkicking foot to continue the movement (1.75).

1.72

1.73

1.74

1.75

Ground Control & Turning—Outside of the Foot

To control with the outside of the foot, the player must first calculate the pace of the ball. This will determine whether to go meet it. If the player judges to stay, because the ball has been played firmly, then the receiving player will only have to redirect it by using the outside of the foot while turning (1.76). If the player goes forward to meet the ball, the nonkicking foot should be planted alongside it as the turning foot is extended forward to make contact. This foot should be raised and pointed inward so that it redirects the path of the ball with the outside of the foot (1.77), enabling the player to control and turn in one movement (1.78, 1.79).

1.76

1.77

1.79

1.78

Common Faults

- Taking eyes off the ball.
- Not getting in line with the ball.
- Selecting the wrong turning surface.
- Stiff joints.
- Failure to keep close control.

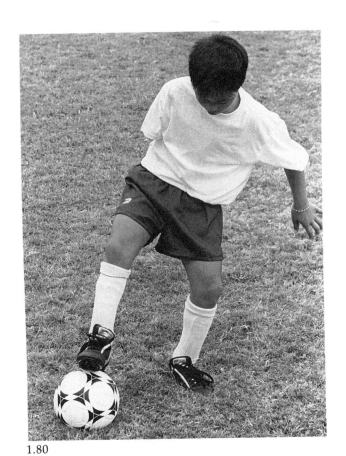

1.80

Ground Control—Sole of the Foot

When using the sole of the foot to control the ball, the player should move forward to trap it with the ball of the foot (1.80). The controlling leg should be bent and the foot held at a 45 degree angle to the ground. After contact the player must keep the weight on the noncontrolling leg to maintain balance.

Aerial Control—Inside of the Foot

A method of controlling a ball of medium height and flight path is to use the inside of the foot. With eyes on the ball the player should move the controlling surface into its line of flight (1.81). Keeping the body in an upright position and the arms out for balance, the nonkicking foot should be pointing towards the direction of the ball. The controlling leg should be lifted and turned out from the hip, forward of the player, so that when contact is made it can be withdrawn (1.82). The ankle joint should be locked to take the pace off the ball and ensure that it drops down. The point of contact with the inside of the foot should be through the midline of the ball.

1.81

1.82

Aerial Control—Instep

With the head steady and eyes fixed firmly, the player should move into and underneath the line of flight of the ball. The controlling leg should be raised from the hip with the toe pointing away, ankle relaxed and the knee bent (1.83).

Contact with the ball and instep should be made about knee height. The noncontrolling leg should be bent slightly at the knee and the arms held out for balance (1.84). The controlling leg should descend rapidly, moving downwards in the beginning almost at the same pace as the ball. As it gets nearer to the ground the speed of descent should be slower.

This will allow the longest possible contact with the instep and ensure that the pace will be taken off the ball.

Aerial Control—Thigh

The player must get underneath and in line with the ball, raise the controlling leg from the hip and bend the knee. If the flight path of the ball is relatively low, the position of the thigh should point obliquely to the ground. If the ball is falling from a higher trajectory then the thigh should be moved into a horizontal poisition (1.85). The soft or upper part of the thigh should make contact with the ball before being withdrawn (1.86). Because of the density of the upper thigh, this will take the pace off the ball. The noncontrolling leg should be slightly bent and the player's eyes fixed firmly on the ball with the arms out for balance.

1.86

1.83

1.84

1.85

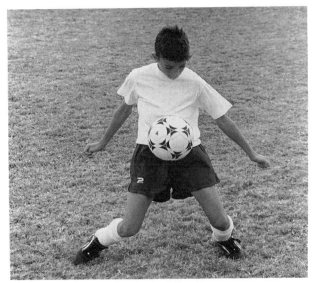

1.87

Aerial Control—Lower Abdomen

Once in line with the flight of the ball, the player can use the stomach or abdomen to control awkward bouncing balls from the ground (1.87).

In most cases a player can apply this technique when reflexes or reactions are too slow to read the bounce.

At the moment of the contact the stomach should be firm with the legs straight while at the same time the upper part of the body leans forward from the hips and over the ball. The arms should be held down to the side and away from the body.

Aerial Control—Chest

When controlling the ball with the chest, the plane of the chest is dependent on the arc of the ball. If the ball is driven hard and straight, the player should move into the line of the flight (1.88), allowing the chest to pull away, cushioning the impact (1.89).

If the ball is dropping from a high arc a wide stance should be taken, allowing the player's chest to get into a horizontal position. Keeping the eyes on the ball the player should move the controlling surface underneath and into its line of flight (1.90). A wide stance will allow the player to bend the knees, push forward with the hips and lean back, positioning the chest to receive the ball (1.91). The arms should be out for balance.

1.88

1.91

1.89

1.90

1.92

1.93

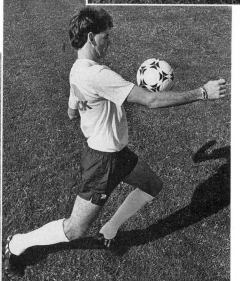

1.94

As a guide the player can use the chin to line up the ball and chest correctly (1.92). As the ball drops, have it aiming at the chin, then at the last moment pull the head back (1.93). The ball should land correctly on the chest. Once contact has been made the ball should be brought to the ground as quickly as possible (1.94, 1.95, 1.96). The angle of impact and rebound are identical while performing this technique.

1.96

1.95

TACKLING

Tackling is a technical and tactical tool in the game of soccer. The technique of tackling is taking the ball directly away from an opponent. The tactical element is the continual consideration of *when to tackle* and *how to tackle*. In some cases the defender may have to delay the opponent and wait for a chance to win the ball.

When tackling the defender should be positioned about a yard from the attacker, using a staggered stance. The foot should be swung backwards as in kicking with the inside of the foot, except that the backswing is shorter (1.97). As the foot comes forward the muscles and joints should be tightened, and the foot placed in front of the ball to act as an obstacle.

When the foot makes contact with the ball, the trunk should be inclined slightly forward and balance maintained by the arms. In order to tackle more powerfully, the tackling foot should be pushed forward on contact.

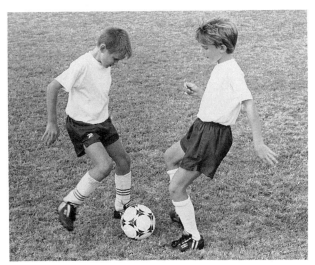

1.97

Common Faults

- Diving in and mistiming.
- Too far away from the opponent when making the tackle.
- Too close to the opponent before making the tackle.
- Nonaggressiveness in the tackle.

HEADING

Heading is an important technique which every outfield player should master. When heading, the player should use the forehead, and nod firmly through the ball in the direction of the target. *Do not allow the ball to just hit the head.*

Heading—Feet on the Ground

When heading from the ground the player should arch the body and firm the neck (1.98). The feet should be spaced apart forming a good base, with the eyes fixed on the ball until impact. The mouth should be closed with the arms out for balance and protection. The trunk should move forward to give strength to the heading action and the forehead should meet the ball hard, putting power into the header (1.99).

1.98

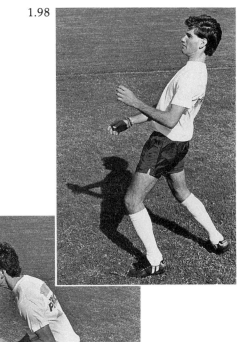

1.99

Point of contact between the head and the ball can vary depending on whether the player is in an attacking or defending situation. If heading to score—*attacking*—the point of contact between the forehead and the ball should be above and through the midline to keep the ball down (1.100).

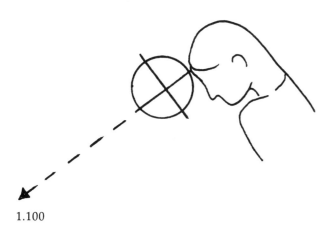

1.100

If heading to clear—*defending*—the point of contact should be below the midline allowing the player height, distance and time (1.101).

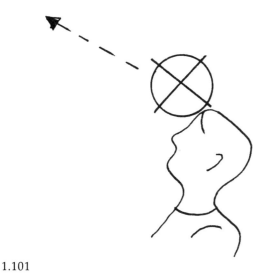

1.101

If the player intends to head the ball sideways, the trunk should be rotated in the required direction so that the surface of the forehead and the trunk are at a right angle, towards the direction that the player wishes the ball to go.

Heading—Feet off the Ground

When the ball has to be headed with the feet off the ground the player can use either of the following methods:

- Running one-footed takeoff.
- Standing two-footed takeoff.

If the player is going to use these the considerations are:

- Timing of the jump.
- Heading the ball at the highest point in the jump.

Heading—One-Footed Takeoff

When using a running one-footed takeoff, the player should use an approach run of five to eight yards. During the run up, it is important that the player does not change pace, as this will cause loss of both speed in the approach and height in the jump.

On takeoff the knee and ankle of the takeoff leg should push upwards and straighten out. The arms should come through and up with the nontakeoff leg bent at the knee and driving upwards.

The action of the arms and nontakeoff leg will aid the player to achieve maximum height. At the point of takeoff the upper body should be leaning forward.

When the player reaches maximum height, the body should lean backwards, then move forward. With the eyes focused on the ball and the neck firm, the forehead should meet the ball with a thrusting action; this will provide the follow-through, and the player should land on both feet.

If the player is heading in an *attacking* situation, the ball should be struck *above* the midline, enabling it to be played downwards. For *defending* purposes the ball must be headed *below* the midline to achieve distance, height, and time.

Common Faults

- Mistiming the jump.
- Failure to keep the eyes on the ball.
- Incorrect surface.

Heading—Two-Footed Takeoff

The player should start the jumping action by planting the feet, either staggered or parallel, 8–10 inches apart. The arms should be swung backwards and the knees slightly bent with the upper body leaning forward.

The arms should then be swung forwards and upwards with the legs straightening out and the feet pushing off the ground (1.102). The upper body should move backwards and then thrust forward to allow the forehead to meet the ball (1.103). The player should end up landing on both feet.

If the player intends changing the direction of the ball, the trunk should be rotated towards the intended direction of play immediately after takeoff (1.104).

1.104

1.102

1.103

GOALKEEPING

The dictionary defines the word "goalkeeper" in the following manner:

> In some cases a player who is stationed at a goal to block the ball.

Certainly keeping the ball out of the net is the primary objective, but there is more to goalkeeping than just stopping shots.

Communication and organization of the players in the team are two of the hidden strengths that a goalkeeper can use to help prevent dangerous situations from developing. The goalkeeper's ability to read these situations is not always appreciated, as all that people see are the shots that are saved—and not saved.

Being the only team member allowed to use hands as well as feet, the goalkeeper must possess the athleticism of a gymnast (1.105), be the last line of defense and the instigator of attacks. It is therefore surprising that despite requiring all of these attributes goalkeepers are often neglected during coaching sessions.

Here we illustrate that there is no mystery to goalkeeping; efficiency is based on correct decision-making and technique.

1.106

Starting Position

The goalkeepers feet should be shoulder width apart, the knees slightly bent which will bring the body weight forward onto the front part of the feet (1.106). The arms and hands should be outside the line of the body and waist high. The head should be steady and tilted slightly forward with the eyes fixed firmly on the ball.

1.105

Basic Handling—Ground Shots

When the goalkeeper has time to get the whole body behind the ball there are *two basic techniques for stopping ground shots:*

Stoop Technique. The feet should be directly behind the ball, close enough together not to allow the ball to go through the legs (1.107). The arms should be down with the hands behind the ball and the palms facing outwards to enable the ball to be scooped upwards and into the chest (1.108). The head should be steady with the eyes on the ball.

Kneeling Technique. The feet and lower body should be sideways onto the ball with the knee of the kneeling leg alongside the heel of the other leg. The trunk should be turned so that the shoulders are facing square on towards the ball (1.109). The arms should be down with the hands behind the ball and the palms facing outwards. Head should be steady with the eyes on the ball (1.110). With this technique the goalkeeper should be able to scoop the ball into the chest and stand up (1.111, 1.112). However, if balance is lost the goalkeeper should drop forward, pinning the ball towards the ground between the arms and the chest. (1.113).

1.107

1.108

1.113

1.112

1.109

1.110

1.111

40

Handling—Waist High Shots

The starting position is as described above with the head steady and the eyes on the ball. The palms of the hands should be facing outwards to cup the ball into the waist (1.114), while the upper body folds over to secure it (1.115).

1.115

1.114

Handling—Chest Shots

The starting position is as described above with the head steady and the eyes on the ball. The palms of the hands should be facing outwards to cup the ball into the chest. On impact the chest should be relaxed so that the ball can be trapped firmly between the hands and chest (1.116).

1.116

Handling—Head-High & Above Shots

The starting position is as described above with the head steady and the eyes fixed firmly on the ball. The hands should be behind and to the side of the ball. The fingers should be spread and relaxed forming a "W" formation (1.117).

Once the ball has been caught, it should be brought quickly down into the body to protect it from opponents. When handling shots above the head the goalkeeper should push upwards off one leg to gain maximum height in the jump and give protection against a challenge from opponents (1.118).

1.117

1.118

1.119

1.120

1.122

Diving—Shots Near the Body

These are difficult to save, especially if they are on the ground. The leg closest to the ball should collapse quickly (1.119), enabling the lower body to get out of the way so that the upper part and hands can stop the ball (1.120).

Diving—Shots Away From the Body

The correct technique is to move the body weight onto the leg nearest the ball and thrust off that leg when making the save (1.121).

1.121

Diving—Vision

To avoid obstruction of vision, the goalkeeper should dive sideways-on with the arms positioned so that they are outside the line of vision (1.122). Do not allow the goalkeeper to dive face down, as this will impair vision.

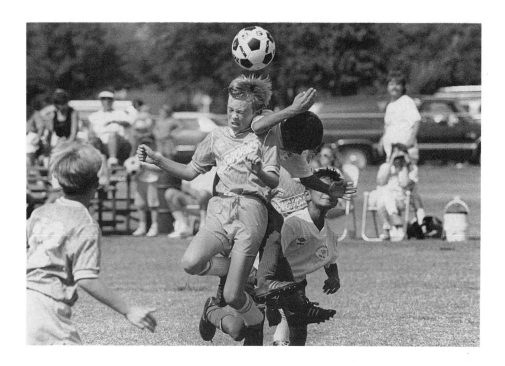

II

INJURY MANAGEMENT

Our intent with this chapter is to help lessen the chance of injuries to players as well as provide basic first-aid procedures. A collision in the sport of soccer can sometimes result in injury. Preventative measures are a major part of any sport and should be incorporated into your program. Maintaining fluids, guarding against and recognizing heat illnesses, and providing adequate warm-up through stretching are important methods of preventing problems that could become acute.

STRETCHING

Stretching is important prior to strenuous activity and is essential to prevent injury.

Players Should Warm Up by engaging in light exercise with the ball to maximize practice time.

This will increase the blood flow to the muscles as well as warm and prepare them for stretching. Never stretch a cold muscle. Once the body is sweating freely, all major muscle groups should be stretched.

- **Quadriceps.** (2.1).
- **Hamstrings.** (2.2, 2.3).
- **Groins.** (2.4).
- **Calves.** (2.5).
- **Lower Back.** (2.6, 2.7, 2.8).

Never use any rubs or icy-hot rubs on an injured muscle. This will cause increased swelling and decreased range of motion.

2.1 **Quadriceps**

Hamstrings

2.2

2.3

2.4 **Groins**

Before practice or a game a light stretching regimen should be followed once the body is sweating freely, and also afterwards to cool the body down. This will help increase flexibility and decrease muscle soreness and tightness.

2.5 **Calves**

2.8

Lower Back

2.7

2.6

FLUIDS

Before training or games, the body should be pre-hydrated by drinking eight to ten cups of water. This will saturate the body tissues and give the body a reserve to draw from as it perspires. Remember that when the body sweats, it loses more than just water; it loses iron, trace minerals, and calcium. These are important to the muscles to keep them functioning normally.

Electrolyte drinks will also replace these essential elements, but they should only be used during periods of inactivity as they have a tendency to upset the stomach when engaging in intense exercise.

During the match or practice, water should be supplied every 15–20 minutes to avoid dehydration. Cold water is a must, because it is absorbed into the tissues faster than tepid water. When it is very humid, fluids must be replaced even more frequently.

HEAT ILLNESSES

Heat Cramps are the first sign of dehydration. Any player who suffers cramps should be removed from the field immediately and encouraged to drink cold fluids. Lightly stretching and massaging the muscles involved will help to alleviate the problem more quickly.

Heat Exhaustion is a serious condition; the person may seem disoriented and will sweat profusely. The skin will become flushed.

Heat Stroke is a *medical emergency.* The kidneys will shut down; the skin will be dry and clammy. The person will be disoriented or unconscious and should be taken to hospital immediately.

For All Heat Illnesses the person should be given cold fluids unless unconscious. Ice bags or cold towels should be put behind the neck, under armpits, on elbows, and behind the knees.

Restrictive clothing should be loosened or removed to allow air to get to the skin. A cool damp cloth should be rubbed over the skin to promote evaporation.

NOSE BLEEDS

Besides impact, nose bleeds can be caused by a combination of overheating and dehydration. The person should be placed in a shaded or air-conditioned area. Blood flow can be restricted by pinching the bridge of the nose (2.9). Place a pad under the nose to catch the blood. Do not tilt the head back; this causes the blood to drain into the stomach, causing nausea. Place an ice pack over the nose to quicken blood-clotting.

2.9

SHIN SPLINTS

Shin splints are characterized by very sharp, shooting pains down the shins. This condition has a slow onset but becomes debilitating. Rest and ice are the most important aids in overcoming this injury.

Preventing Shin Splints can be helped by supporting the arch and stretching the calves.

FLESH WOUNDS

Simple Abrasion is best treated by washing the area with soap and water, and leaving it open.

Laceration is treated by placing a sterile gauze pad or clean cloth over the wound and applying direct pressure to slow the bleeding. Ice will also help the blood to clot.

Do Not Use a Tourniquet as this will cut off the blood supply which causes tissue to die.

SUSPECT THE WORST

The most important concept, is always *suspect the worst* in the event of an injury.

Splints. If an injury occurs requiring a splint, immobilize the area using anything from two boards to a couple of rolled-up newspapers. Commercial splints are preferable if available.

Rest. Keep the weight off the injured area to prevent complicating the injury.

Ice. Apply an ice pack to the area. Remember, ice packs should never be applied directly to the skin. A damp cloth should cover the area to prevent frostbite.

Ice should always be used on a new injury as it will slow down the swelling by reducing the blood flow to the area. Ice should **not** be used on an **old injury** before activity.

Ice should be applied for a minimum of 15 minutes to 20 minutes. Before reapplying the ice, allow 20–30 minutes for the area to warm-up again. Ice treatment should continue for up to 72 hours after the injury. All swelling should be over by this time.

The R.I.C.E. Principle is an easy acronym to remember:

Rest. To avoid further complications.

Ice. To control pain and swelling.

Compression. To compress swelling.

Elevation. To control the blood flow.

KEEP A FIRST-AID KIT NEARBY

Have a medical kit stocked with at least these rudimentary items:

- Ice
- Ice chest
- Plastic bags
- Assorted Band-Aids
- Antiseptic solution
- Antibiotic ointment
- Scissors
- Gauze
- Soap
- Tweezers
- Clean water
- Splint materials
- Sunscreen
- Athletic tape

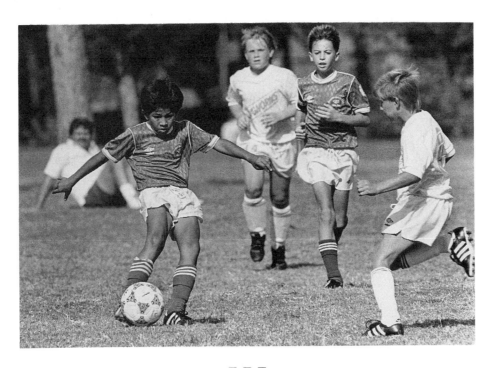

III
U-8 DRILLS & PRACTICES
(under age 8)

At this age level, focus team play on small-sided games; one-on-one through three-on-three. Place the emphasis on active, fun soccer allowing many touches on the ball while introducing and developing basic techniques—dribbling, kicking, control, and heading.

Once every four weeks expose each of the players to the goalkeeping position. This will help each player develop an overall, well-balanced perspective of the goalkeeper's role.

Length of Training Session: 40–60 Minutes

- **Warm-up.** 10 minutes

- **Technique Introduction.** 10 minutes

- **Skill Development.** 10 minutes

- **Team Game.** 10–15 minutes

- **Free Play.** 10–20 minutes

PRACTICES

Warm-up

3.1

Field Size. 15-yd × 15-yd grid.

Organization. 10 players, each with a soccer ball, four cones. All the players are dribbling their ball inside the grid (3.1). The coach shouts a part of the body that each player has to use to stop the ball—e.g., sole of the right foot, the left knee, etc.

Coaching Points

- Do not allow players to run in straight lines or circles.
- Encourage players to zigzag.
- Keep the players moving.
- Head up.
- Close control.
- No toe-kicking.

Warm-up

3.2

Field Size. 20-yd × 20-yd grid.

Organization. 10 players, groups of two, with one soccer ball per group. Have each group pass and receive with the inside of the foot (3.2).

Progression. Restrict players to two touches.

Coaching Points

- Use the correct kicking surface.
- Get in line to receive the ball.
- Move after the pass.
- Accuracy—weight and timing of the pass.

3.3

Field Size. 20-yd × 20-yd grid.

Organization. 10 players, each with a soccer ball, four cones. Everyone dribbles around the grid (3.3). The objective: the players try to kick everyone else's soccer ball out of the grid, while keeping their own ball protected.

Dribbling

Field Size. 40-yd × 40-yd grid.

Organization. 10 players, groups of two, one soccer ball per group, 14 cones. Use 10 cones to make five small goals, 1½ yards wide (3.4). Put a group at each goal and have them play one-on-one, dribbling towards the group's own central goal. The pairs can score through either side of their own goal.

3.4

Dribbling

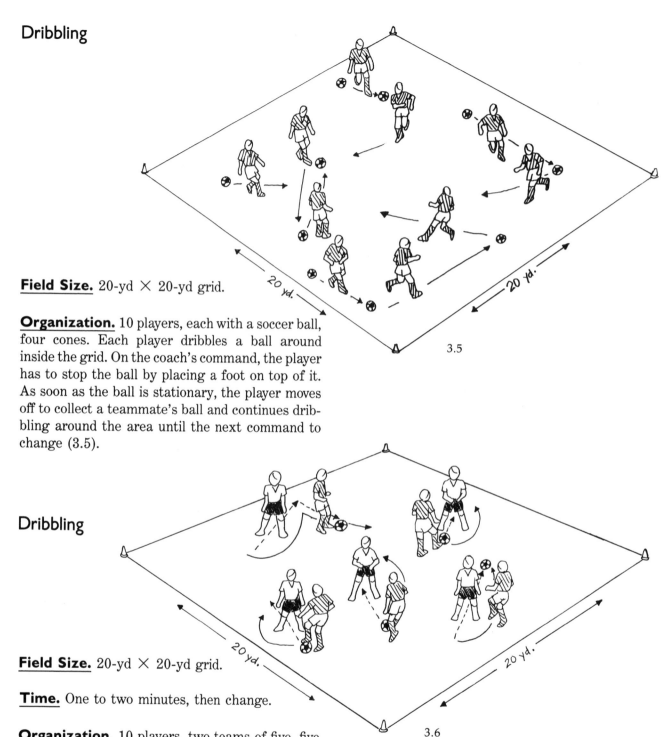

3.5

Field Size. 20-yd × 20-yd grid.

Organization. 10 players, each with a soccer ball, four cones. Each player dribbles a ball around inside the grid. On the coach's command, the player has to stop the ball by placing a foot on top of it. As soon as the ball is stationary, the player moves off to collect a teammate's ball and continues dribbling around the area until the next command to change (3.5).

Dribbling

3.6

Field Size. 20-yd × 20-yd grid.

Time. One to two minutes, then change.

Organization. 10 players, two teams of five, five soccer balls, five bibs. One team, without soccer balls, stands anywhere inside the grid, with legs apart. The other team's players each have a soccer ball. On the coach's command each player with a soccer ball is to dribble and play the ball through the legs of the other team's players (3.6). Each time a player does this, a point is awarded. The object is to see how many points each team can accumulate during the allotted time. The only restriction is that the dribbling player cannot go back through the same set of legs without going through another set.

50

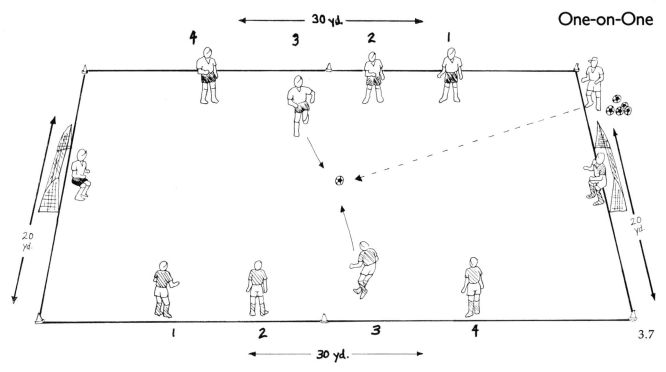

3.7

Field Size. 30 yd × 20 yd.

Organization. 10 players, two teams of five—four outfield players and one goalkeeper—six cones, five bibs. Keepers should be rotated every 10 shots. Each outfield player should be numbered 1–4. The coach plays the ball between the two teams and shouts a number; the designated player on each team runs out and battles to win the ball, with the winner attempting to dribble and score (3.7).

Coaching Points

- Head up, awareness of other players.
- Close control.
- Bend the knees.
- Change of direction.
- Change of pace.
- Feinting.

Passing—Inside of the foot (Individual)

3.8

Organization. One player, one soccer ball. From a distance of five to ten yards kick or pass the ball against a wall using the inside of the foot. Attempt to keep the ball below an imaginary line with consecutive passes (3.8). Variations on this theme can be achieved by using the instep or outside of the foot.

Passing—Inside of the foot

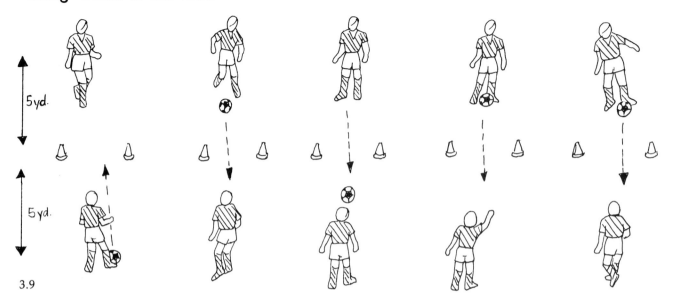

5 yd.

5 yd.

3.9

Organization. 10 players in groups of two, one soccer ball per group, 10 cones. The practice is set up where two cones are placed two yards apart, with each player five yards from the cones. Both players must pass the ball back and forth through the cones using two touches (3.9). After achieving some proficiency, turn the practice into a game, where each group of two plays against all the other groups, e.g., see how many successful passes can be made in one minute. All passes must go through the cones cleanly.

Passing—Inside of the foot

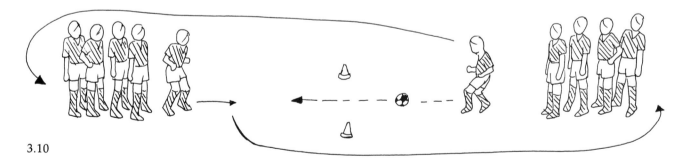

3.10

Organization. 10 players, two groups of five, one soccer ball, two cones. Place the cones two yards apart in the middle and the two groups of five on each side of the cones; play the ball through the cones using two touches. The player follows the pass to the other line (3.10). To make this into a competitive game have the teams complete a number of successful passes against the clock, e.g., 20 passes in three minutes.

3.11

Organization. 10 players, five groups of two, one soccer ball per group, 11 cones. Set up five grids, 10 yds × 10 yds. Have a group in each grid passing and moving; keep the ball inside the grid, using the inside of the foot (3.11).

Coaching Points

- Approach the ball in a straight line.
- Nonkicking foot slightly behind the ball and pointing at the target.
- The kicking leg should be bent with the swing action coming from the hip, ankle locked and the toe pointed away to the side.
- Head down, strike through the middle or top half of the ball to keep it low.
- Arms out for balance.

Passing—Outside of the foot

3.12

Field Size. 50 yds × 20 yds.

Organization. 10 players, five soccer balls, 22 cones. Each player has a partner with one ball between two. Pass the ball through the cones set out two yards apart, using the outside of the foot.

Start the practice with the players five to six yards away from the cones and increase the distance as the players become more successful (3.12).

Passing—Outside of the foot

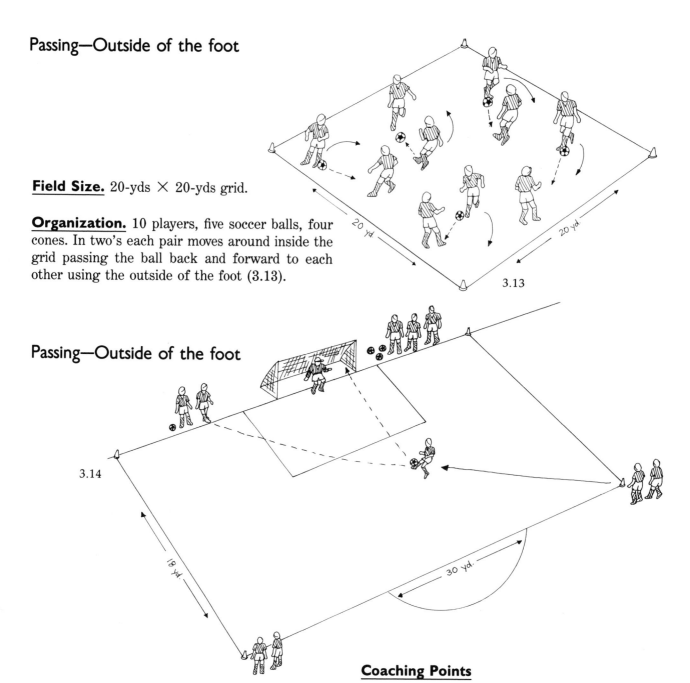

Field Size. 20-yds × 20-yds grid.

Organization. 10 players, five soccer balls, four cones. In two's each pair moves around inside the grid passing the ball back and forward to each other using the outside of the foot (3.13).

3.13

Passing—Outside of the foot

3.14

Organization. 10 players plus a goalkeeper, five soccer balls, four cones. Five players on the goal line, the others along the edge of the penalty area. Goalkeeper in goal. Working in pairs the player on the goal line plays a ball diagonally across the penalty area to a partner who strikes the ball using the outside of the foot in an attempt to score. Following the shot the player retrieves the ball while the passer advances to the edge of the penalty area (3.14).

Coaching Points

- Nonkicking foot 8–10 inches from the ball slightly behind it.
- Kicking foot pointed down and inwards.
- Kicking foot knee bent, and kicking action from the hip.
- Strike ball off center.
- Head down, body over the ball to keep the ball low.

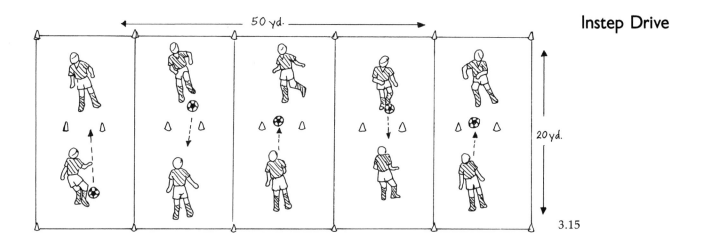

3.15

Field Size. 50 yds × 20 yds.

Organization. 10 players, 22 cones, five soccer balls, one ball between two. Each player attempts to play the ball through two cones spaced two yards apart, using the instep drive. Starting distance from the cones should be approximately five to six yards, increasing to 10 yards as progress is made (3.15).

Instep Drive

3.16

Organization. 10 players plus a goalkeeper, five soccer balls, seven cones. Place the cones in an arc approximately 10 yards from goal. Five teams of two are selected. One player from each pair should be situated at the goal post with the ball and the other behind the first set of cones in the arc. Using the inside of the foot, the player on the post passes the ball between each set of cones in turn; the other partner attempts to score with an instep drive (3.16). Each time a score is made the successful two proceed to the next area.

Instep Drive

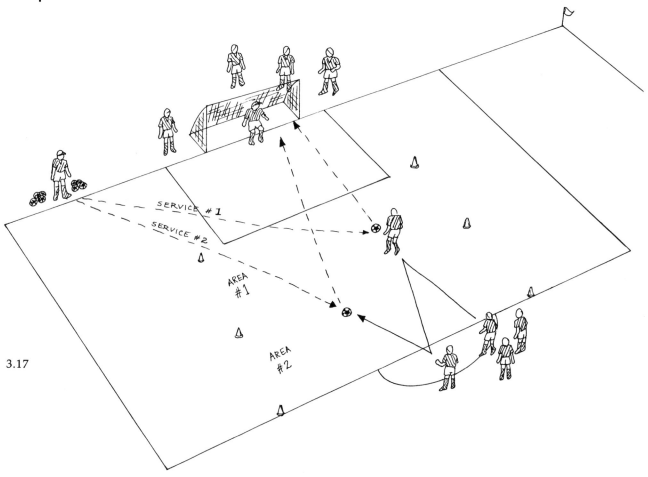

3.17

Organization. Nine players plus a goalkeeper, 10 soccer balls, six cones. The coach's position should be alongside the goal with the soccer balls. All of the players with the exception of the goalkeeper should be stationed outside the "D" of the penalty area (3.17). The coach plays a ball into area #1. One player advances forward and tries to score with an instep drive. Following the attempt, the player returns to the top of the "D" as the coach delivers another pass, this time into area. #2. The player should try again to score with the instep drive. If unsuccessful with both shots, the player goes behind the goal to assist in retrieving balls. If successful in scoring one attempt, the player may go back to the group and wait another turn. If a player scores twice, the player can nominate a

teammate to come forward; the nominated player must score both times otherwise they also have to help retrieve the balls from behind the goal.

Coaching Points

- Angle of approach.
- Head down.
- Nonkicking foot behind and to the side of the ball pointing at the target.
- Kicking action from the hip, knee slightly bent and over the ball, ankle locked with the toe pointing down.
- Contact made with the shoelaces.
- Land on the shooting foot.

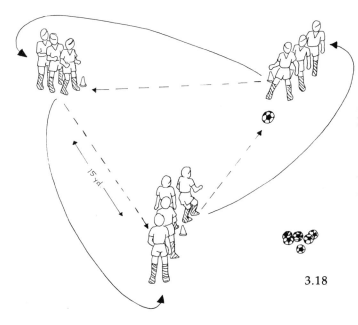

3.18

Organization. 10 players split into two groups of three and one group of four with one soccer ball. The three groups form a triangle 15 yds × 15 yds × 15 yds. The group of four commence the practice with the ball. A player passes the ball and follows the pass to the back of the other line (3.18).

Field Size. 10-yd × 10-yd grid.

Organization. 10 players, split into four groups, two of two and two of three, one soccer ball per group, four cones. The groups of three should commence the practice passing the ball with the inside of the foot and following the pass. The receiving players should control with the inside of the foot, return the ball and follow it (3.19). A competitive game can be made by playing the two groups against each other or the two groups against the clock, e.g., completing a predetermined number of passes within a given time frame.

3.19

3.20

Organization. 10 players, two groups of five, one soccer ball, and five cones per group. Place the cones in a zigzag formation approximately 12 yards apart with a player in front of each cone. Each group must pass the ball back and forth in the zigzag formation (3.20). Make a competitive game by playing one group against the other.

Ground Control

Organization. 10 players, two groups of five form two circles, one ball per circle.

Call the name of the intended receiver, pass and follow the ball then fill the space left by that player. The receiver comes and collects the ball and repeats the exercise (3.21).

Coaching Points

- Get in line with the ball.
- Come to meet the ball.
- Make an early decision on which foot surface to use.
- Be relaxed on contact.

3.21

Aerial Control

Organization. The player throws the ball up in the air and lets the ball bounce (3.22, 3.23). After the bounce the player can use any of the six controlling surfaces: either foot, either thigh, chest, head.

3.22

3.23

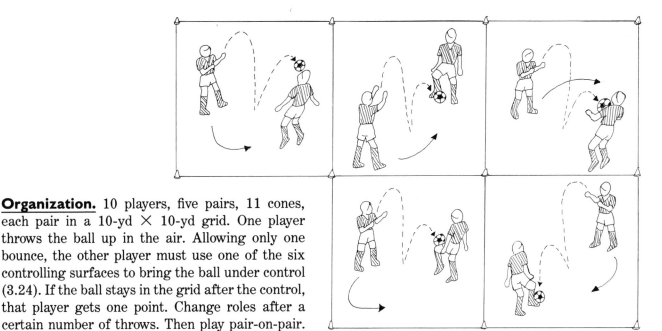

Organization. 10 players, five pairs, 11 cones, each pair in a 10-yd × 10-yd grid. One player throws the ball up in the air. Allowing only one bounce, the other player must use one of the six controlling surfaces to bring the ball under control (3.24). If the ball stays in the grid after the control, that player gets one point. Change roles after a certain number of throws. Then play pair-on-pair.

3.24

Aerial Control

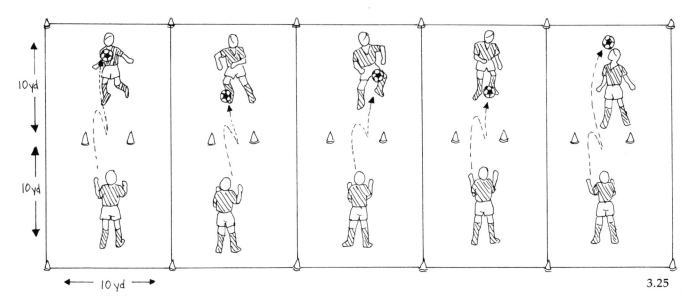

10 yd

10 yd

← 10 yd →

3.25

Organization: 10 players, five pairs, five soccer balls, 22 cones. The player with the ball serves it underhand so it will bounce in the partner's grid. This player can use any one of the six controlling surfaces and must control the ball after the first bounce, then on the second or third touch, must play the ball back through the cones to the partner (3.25).

59

Aerial Control

Field Size. 10-yd × 10-yd grid.

Organization. Players in groups of three, two soccer balls per group. One of the end players serves the ball underhand to a receiving player. The receiver controls using any one of the six controlling surfaces and plays the ball back to the same server. The receiver then turns and controls a ball from another serving player, and repeats the exercise (3.26). After a period of time, change the players around until each has had a turn at receiving. Keep the ball in the grid.

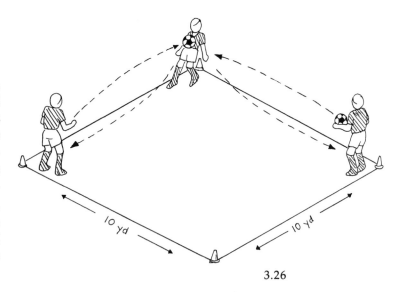

10 yd

10 yd

3.26

Aerial Control

Field Size. 10-yd × 10-yd grid.

Organization. Players in groups of three, one soccer ball per group. The player with the ball serves underhand to the receiving player. The receiving player then controls and turns, using one of the six controlling surfaces and plays the ball to the other player who picks it up and repeats the exercise (3.27).

Coaching Points

- Get in line and underneath the ball.
- Make an early decision on which controlling surface to use.
- Be relaxed on contact.

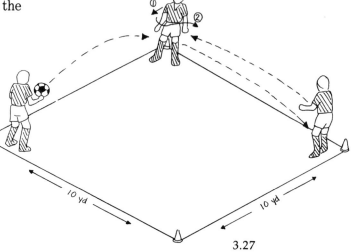

10 yd

10 yd

3.27

Heading (Individual)

① ② 3.28

Organization. The player throws the soccer ball lightly up into the air and attempts to juggle it on the head (3.28). With this age group the coach may want to use a *rubber ball* or a *soft soccer ball* to help reduce the fear factor.

3.29

3.30

Organization. 10 players, in pairs, one soccer ball per pair. The receiving player sits down (3.29, 3.30, 3.31). The serving player stands five yards away and serves the ball underhand for the receiver to head back. The sitting player should keep the trunk upright and the neck stiff. The arms are pulled back to increase power in the header. After a certain number of headers change the players around.

Heading

3.31

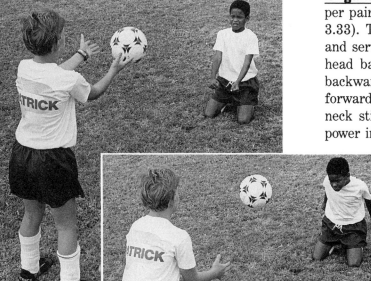

3.32

3.33

Organization. 10 players, in pairs, one soccer ball per pair. The receiving player kneels down (3.32, 3.33). The serving player stands five yards away and serves the ball underhand for the receiver to head back. The kneeling player should be tilted backwards, not sitting on the legs, and should rock forward from the hips keeping the upper torso and neck stiff. The arms are pulled back to increase power in the header.

Coaching Points

- Move forward to meet the ball.
- Arch body and snap forward for maximum power.
- Ensure contact is made with the forehead.
- Eyes should be open and mouth closed.

Goalkeeping
(Basic handling, Ground, Stoop Technique)

Organization. Goalkeepers in pairs, one soccer ball per pair. Goalkeepers standing 10 yards apart facing each other. Each keeper takes a turn at rolling the ball along the ground to the other keeper who collects it in the stoop technique (3.34).

3.34   10 yd.

Goalkeeping
(Basic handling, Ground, Stoop Technique—including footwork)

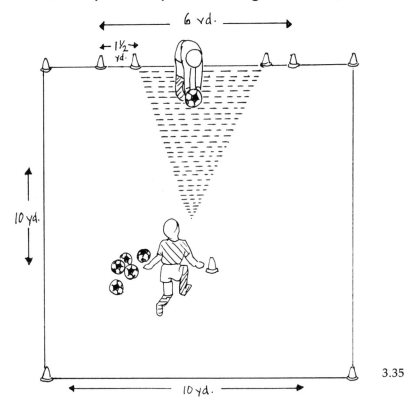

6 yd.

1½ yd.

10 yd.

10 yd.

3.35

Organization. Goalkeepers in pairs using a number of soccer balls. Goals should be marked by placing cones six yards apart; another cone should be placed one-and-one half yards inside each post. The goalkeeper should start in the center of the goal for each service. Balls are rolled along the ground to the shaded area (3.35). The goalkeeper should shuffle sideways to collect the ball, using the stoop technique.

Coaching Points

- Head steady and eyes on the ball.
- Get in line with the ball.
- Ensure short sideways strides as goalkeeper adjusts.
- Hands positioned behind the ball.
- Feet behind the ball and close together.
- Bend from the waist; do not squat.
- Cup ball to the chest.

Organization. Goalkeepers in pairs using a number of soccer balls. Goals should be set up using cones placed six yards apart; another cone should be placed two yards inside each post. A ball should be rolled along the ground to the shaded area (3.36). The goalkeeper should collect the ball in the stoop technique.

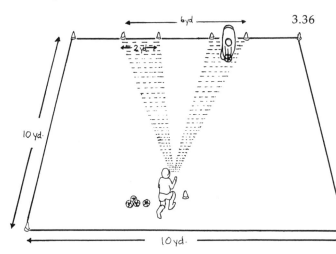

3.36

Goalkeeping (Distribution, Kicking—Volley)

Organization. Goalkeepers in pairs, one soccer ball per pair. Goalkeepers spaced 20 yards apart. The ball should be dropped from the hands and kicked; the partner collects it and returns it in the same manner (3.38).

Coaching Points

- Approach the ball straight on.
- Hold and drop the ball from both hands.
- Head down with eyes on the ball.
- Lean slightly back on contact.
- The ball makes contact with the lace part of the shoe and the toe should be pointed away.

Goalkeeping
(Distribution, Kicking—Dead Ball)

Organization. Goalkeepers in pairs, one soccer ball per pair. Goalkeepers spaced 20 yards apart. The ball should be kicked from the ground; the partner collects it and returns it in the same manner (3.37).

Coaching points

- Same as for a lofted pass.

3.37

3.38

Goalkeeping
(Distribution, Kicking—Half Volley)

20 yd.

3.39

Organization. Goalkeepers in pairs, one soccer ball per pair. Goalkeepers spaced 20 yards apart. The ball should be dropped from both hands and half-volleyed to the partner who collects it and returns it in the same manner (3.39).

Coaching Points

- Approach the ball straight on.
- Hold and drop the ball from both hands.
- Head down with eyes on the ball.
- Lean slightly back on contact.
- The kicking foot makes contact with the ball as it strikes the ground.
- The ball makes contact with the laces part of the shoe.
- Ankle locked and the toe pointed down.

Goalkeeping
(Shot Stopping—Ground)

Step 1   Step 2   Step 3

3 yd.

3.40

Coaching Points

- Head steady, eyes fixed on the ball.
- One hand behind the ball and the other on top of it.
- Keeper should land on side, not on stomach.
- Pull the ball in towards the body to complete the save.

Organization. Goalkeepers in pairs, one soccer ball per pair. Goalkeepers spaced three yards apart. One goalkeeper kneels. The other goalkeeper hand serves the ball by rolling it to the left of the kneeling player, who dives to stop it (3.40). The ball should be returned and the exercise repeated to the right side of the kneeling player. After repeating the exercise six times on each side the players should reverse positions.

3.41

Coaching Points

- Head steady, eyes fixed on the ball.
- Fingers behind and to the side of the ball with thumbs and forefingers forming a "W."
- Keeper should land on side, not on stomach.
- Pull the ball in towards the body to complete the save.
- Ensure that the goalkeeper pushes off with the foot closest to the ball.

Organization. Goalkeepers in pairs, one soccer ball per pair. Goalkeepers spaced three yards apart. One goalkeeper kneels. The other goalkeeper hand serves the ball by throwing it in the air to the left side of the kneeling player who dives to stop it (3.41) The ball should be returned and the exercise repeated to the right side of the kneeling player. After repeating the exercise six times on each side, the players should reverse positions.

3.42

Goalkeeping
(Shot Stopping—Air)

Organization. Goalkeepers in pairs, one soccer ball per pair. Goalkeepers spaced three yards apart. One goalkeeper squats. The other goalkeeper hand serves the ball by throwing it in the air to the left side of the squatting player who springs sideways to make the save (3.42). The ball should be returned and the exercise repeated to the right side of the squatting player. After repeating the exercise six times on each side the players should reverse positions.

Coaching Points

- Head steady, eyes fixed on the ball.
- Fingers behind and to the side of the ball with thumbs and forefingers forming a "W."
- Keeper should land on side, not on stomach.
- Pull the ball in towards the body to complete the save.

TEAM GAMES

Understanding the game is the most important aspect of a player's development. If a player understands why depth or width is important in a small-sided game, the player should be able to adapt freely in a full game.

The *principles of play* can provide the foundation upon which the future development of positional play can take place. Therefore, they should be used as a framework on which all teaching and coaching is developed.

Attack

- **Depth.** Supporting the teammate on the ball, allowing the player to pass it through 360 degrees.

- **Communication.** Provide the player receiving the ball with verbal support so the player has direction (hold, turn, etc.).

- **Penetration.** Moving the ball into or through the opposition defense.

- **Width.** Playing balls into wide positions to draw defenders away from each other.

- **Mobility.** The movement of players in front or behind the player with the ball; therefore affecting the position of defensive players.

- **Improvisation.** Players changing roles or doing the unusual.

Defense

- **Pressure on the ball.** Blocking the opponents way towards goal. Channelling the attacker into nonscoring areas.

- **Depth.** Covering the pressuring player and the space behind.

- **Communication.** The supporting player must give verbal instruction to the pressuring player.

- **Balance.** Covering the supporting player and the space behind.

- **Delay.** Jockeying to allow other defenders time to cover.

- **Control & Restraint.** Defenders not selling themselves in the tackle therefore effecting delay.

For all team games: when the ball goes out of play, restart from the touch line with a kick in.

Field Size. 20 yds × 15 yds.

Organization. Two-on-one (3.43).

When the ball goes out over the goal line the game is always restarted by a goal kick.

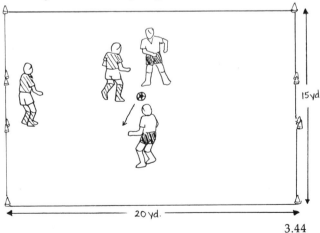

3.44

Field Size. 20 yds × 15 yds.

Organization. Two-on-one plus a goalkeeper (3.44).

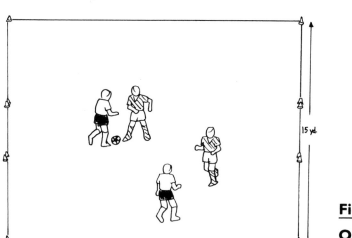

Field Size. 20 yds × 15 yds.

Organization. Two-on-two (3.45).

3.45

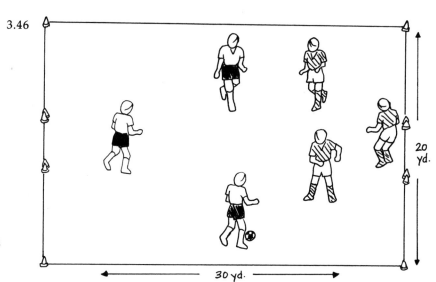

3.46

Field Size. 30 yds × 20 yds.

Organization. Three-on-two plus a goalkeeper (3.46).

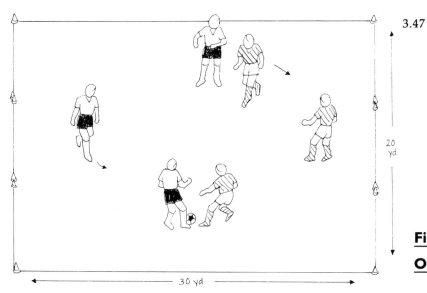

3.47

Field Size. 30 yds × 20 yds.

Organization. Three-on-three (3.47).

U-8 Team Formations

1:1:2:1:2 #1 (3.48)

3.48

1:2:1:1:2 #2 (3.49)

3.49

—IV—
U-10 DRILLS & PRACTICES
(under age 10)

At this age level continue to concentrate team play on small-sided games. Place your emphasis on skill development while encouraging players to spread out.

Length of Training Session: 60 Minutes

- **Warm-up.** 10 minutes
- **Technique/Skill Development.** 20 minutes
- **Team Game.** 10–15 minutes
- **Free Play.** 15–20 minutes

PRACTICES

Warm-up

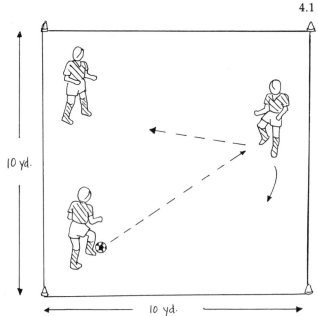

Field Size. 10-yd × 10-yd grids.

Organization. 12 players in four groups of three, four soccer balls, 10 cones.
 The players should pass and move inside their grid using no more than two touches and all foot surfaces to control the ball (4.1).

Shielding

Field Size.
20-yd × 20-yd grid.

Organization. 12 players, nine with a soccer ball. The players without a ball try to kick the soccer balls out from the other players (4.2). This should be done within a time limit.

30 yd.

30 yd.

4.3

Field Size. 30-yd × 30-yd grid.

Organization. Players in pairs, one soccer ball per pair, four cones. The player in possession of the ball shields it while the other player tries to win it (4.3). When this is accomplished the ball is returned. After a time period the roles are reversed. Count the times each player wins the ball.

Coaching Points

- Do not show the ball.
- Keep the ball on the farthest foot.
- Make a long barrier.

Moves—Turns

Field Size. Two 10-yd × 10-yd grids.

Organization. 12 Players, each with a soccer ball, six cones. Each player dribbling a ball around inside the whole grid area (4.4). The coach nominates a grid that the players sprint into with their ball. They continue dribbling there until they receive another command to sprint as before.

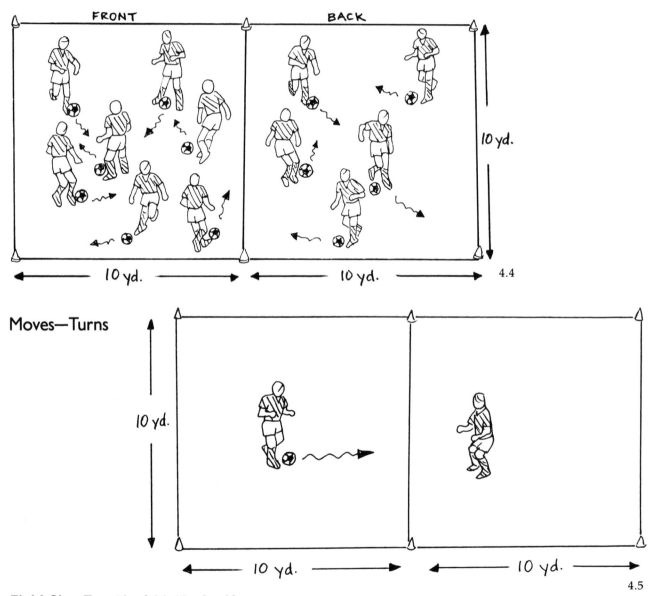

Moves—Turns

Field Size Two 10-yd × 10-yd grids.

Organization. Players in pairs with one soccer ball per pair, six cones. The player with the ball attempts to dribble and carry it over the end line of the grid (4.5). Encourage the attacking player to use different tricks to beat the opponent. Five attempts per player, then change roles.

4.6

4.7

Field Size. 30 yds long.

Organization. 12 Players, four groups of three, one soccer ball per group, eight cones. A player on the outside plays the ball to the player in the middle (4.6). The player in the middle comes to meet the ball, glances over the shoulder before turning with the ball and playing it to the player at the opposite end. Repeat the exercise and encourage players to use different surfaces.

Field Size. 20-yd × 10-yd grid.

Organization. 12 Players, four groups of three, one soccer ball per group, 15 cones. The ball is served to the player in the middle of the grid; this player comes to meet it, glances over the shoulder before turning quickly, attempting to beat the defender while dribbling the ball over the end line (4.7). Repeat the exercise and encourage players to use different turning surfaces and tricks.

Kicking with the Inside of the Foot

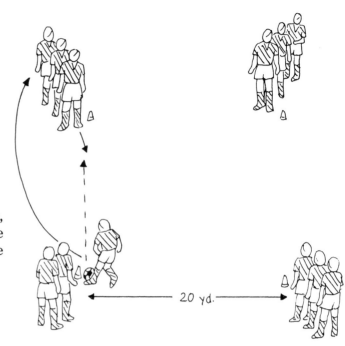

Field Size. 20-yd × 20-yd grid.

Organization. 12 Players, four groups of three, one soccer ball, four cones. One player passes the ball and follows it to any one of the other three groups (4.8). Progress to two touch.

4.8

Kicking with the Inside of the Foot

Step 1   Step 2   Step 3   Step 4

10 yd.

4.9

Field Size. 10-yd × 10yd grids.

Organization. 12 Players, in pairs, one soccer ball per pair, 12 cones. To commence the practice one player passes the ball to the other who controls and takes it around the cone before passing it back, attempting to knock over the partner's cone (4.9).

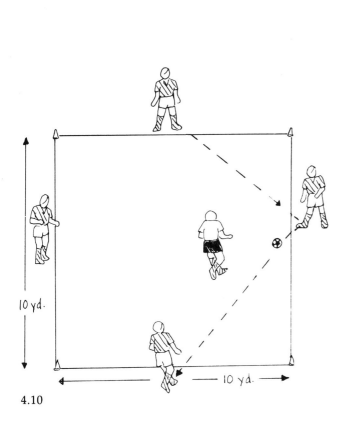

4.10

4.11

Field Size. 10-yd × 10-yd grids.

Organization. Players in groups of five, one soccer ball per group, four cones. Four players are restricted to their side of the grid and must not enter inside. The player in the middle cannot leave the gird (4.10). The object is to pass the ball from the outside diagonally or straight across the grid without the defender intercepting the ball. Should one of the outside players make a mistake such as a bad pass or poor control, then the roles are reversed.

Field Size. 20-yd × 10-yd grids.

Organization. 12 Players in pairs, one soccer ball per group, 14 cones. The ball should be passed between partners using the instep. On receiving, the player controls the ball to the side, then passes it back to the partner who repeats the exercise (4.11). Encourage players to use either foot.

Instep Kicking

4.12

Field Size. 40-yd × 10-yd grids.

Organization. 12 Players in groups of three, one soccer ball per group, 18 cones. To commence the practice a ball is rolled out by the goalkeeper (4.12). The kicker tries to score with an instep drive. If the ball is saved the goalkeeper turns and rolls it to the player on the opposite side. If the kicker scores or the ball goes past, the goalkeeper must recover and anticipate a shot from the player on the opposite side. Keep score and change roles.

Instep Kicking.

4.13

Field Size. 25-yd × 25-yd grid.

Organization. 12 Players in groups of two, one soccer ball per group, eight cones. Partners stand on opposite sides of the grid facing each other, with the object being to knock over the cones in the middle of the grid using an instep drive (4.13).

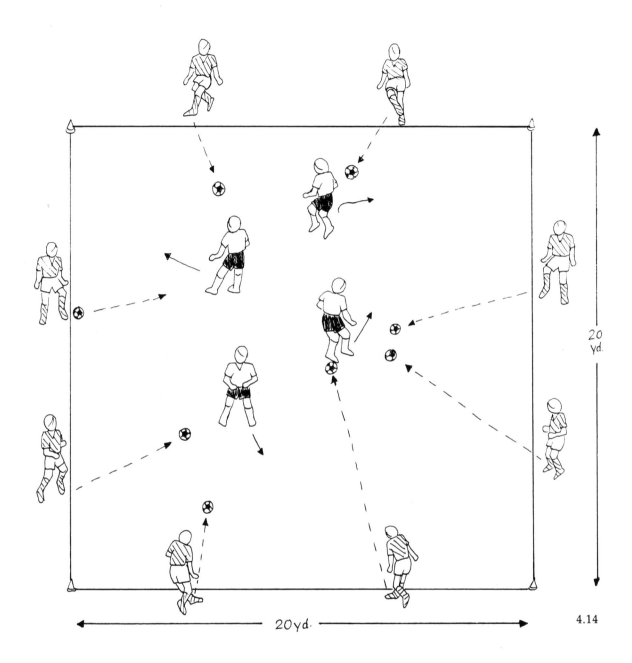

4.14

Field Size. 20-yd × 20-yd grid.

Organization. 12 players, eight balls, four cones. Eight players, each with a soccer ball, stand outside the grid facing the four players on the inside of the grid.

The players with the ball strike it with the outside of the foot and try to hit the players in the middle below the waist (4.14). The kicking player retrieves the ball.

Kicking with the Outside of the Foot

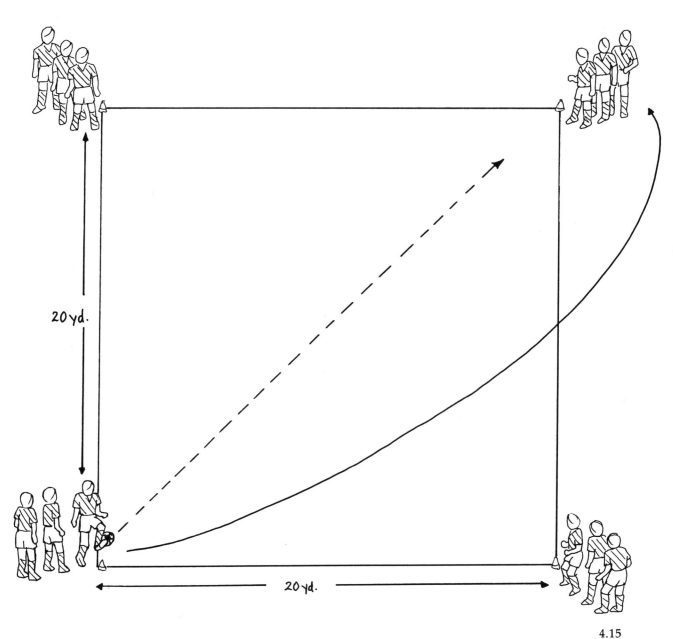

4.15

Field Size. 20-yd × 20-yd grid.

Organization. 12 players, four groups of three, one soccer ball, four cones. Each group is stationed at a cone.

The player with the ball passes it with the outside of the foot to the first player in any one of the other groups, and follows the pass (4.15).

30 yd.

40 yd.

4.16

Field Size. 30-yd × 40-yd grid.

Organization. 12 players in pairs, six soccer balls, four cones. Each pair moves around inside the whole area of the grid, passing the ball to each other using the outside of the foot (4.16). Encourage players to pass with either foot.

Ground Control

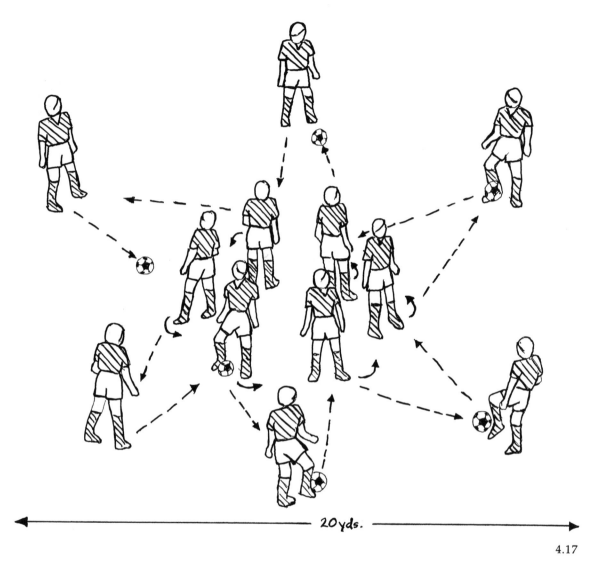

4.17

Field Size. 20-yd × 20-yd grid.

Organization. 12 players in pairs, six soccer balls. The player on the outside passes the ball to a partner in the inside circle. This player controls and returns it before turning left to receive another pass (4.17).

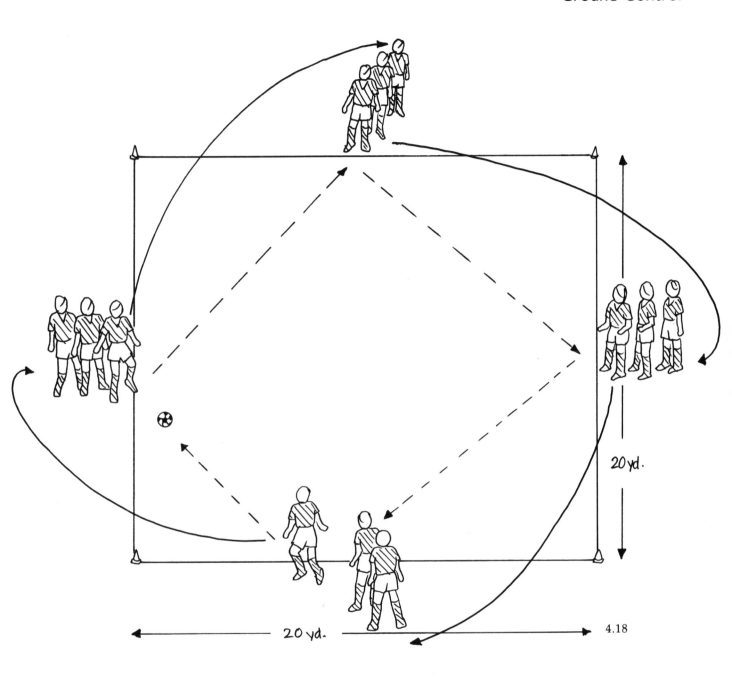

4.18

Field Size. 20-yd × 20-yd grid.

Organization. 12 players in groups of three, one soccer ball, four cones. Each player passes the ball diagonally in a clockwise direction and follows the pass to the back of the group (4.18). Each pass should be controlled with the left foot and passed with the right foot. Then work the practice counterclockwise, reversing the use of the feet.

Ground Control

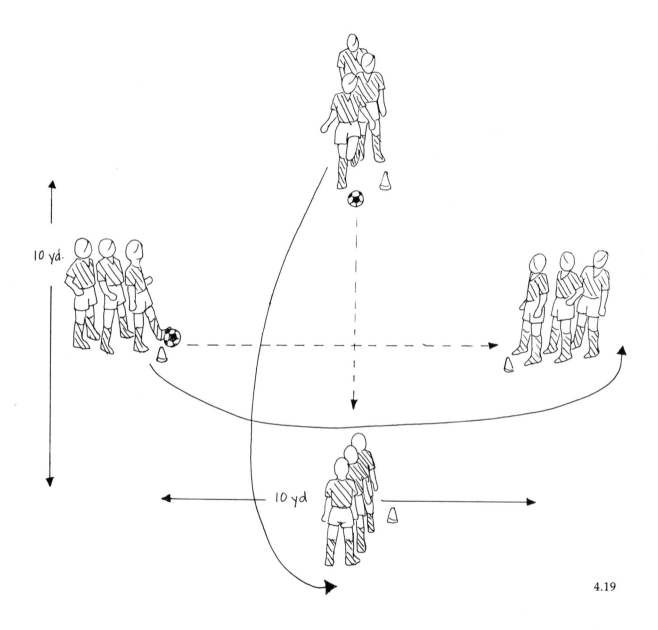

4.19

Field Size. 10-yd × 10-yd grid.

Organization. 12 players in groups of three, two soccer balls, four cones. The first player of each group passes the ball to the first player on the group opposite (4.19). The player follows the pass through to the end of that group. Using no more than two touches to control the ball the pass is returned. During this practice try not to hit the other group's ball.

Step 1

8 yd.

Step 2

4.20

Organization. 12 players in pairs, six soccer balls, 10 cones. Place players eight yards apart. The player with the ball delivers it using a *proper throw-in* (4.20). The receiving player must control the ball with the surface designated by the coach and then pass it back. This practice can be developed so that when the ball is played back the thrower has to control and catch it.

Aerial Control

4.21

5 yd.

Organization. 12 players in pairs, six soccer balls, 10 cones. Place players five yards apart. The first player with the ball delivers it *underhand* (4.21). The receiving player must control it with a surface designated by the coach, let it bounce then pass it back.

Step 1

Step 2

Step 3

5 yd.

4.22

10 yd.

10 yd.

6 yd.

4.23

Field Size. 10-yd × 10-yd grids.

Organization. 12 players in pairs, six soccer balls, 10 cones. Place players five yards apart. The player with the ball delivers it *underhand*; the receiving player must control it with a surface designated by the coach, let it bounce then pass it back (4.22). The first player must now control the ball with a surface designated by the coach and catch it for a point.

Organization. 12 players in pairs, one soccer ball per pair, 12 cones. One pair per grid. To start the practice one player throws the ball in the air and attempts to score a goal by heading it past a partner (4.23). Alternate turns.

4.24

Field Size. 10-yd × 10-yd grids.

Organization. 12 players in pairs, one soccer ball per pair, 12 cones. One pair per grid. To start the practice the player with the ball throws it *underhand* to a partner who attempts to score a goal by heading it back past the serving player (4.24). Alternate turns.

4.25

Organization. 12 players in two groups of six. One player from each group stands by a goal post; the other five members of the group stand 15 yards from goal. The player at the goal post serves the ball so it will bounce; after the bounce the receiving player runs in and heads the ball into the goal (4.25). To score, the ball must hit the goal net on the full (fly). After each attempt the player returns the ball to the server and goes to the back of the line. After the introduction of this practice, play the groups against each other.

Tackling

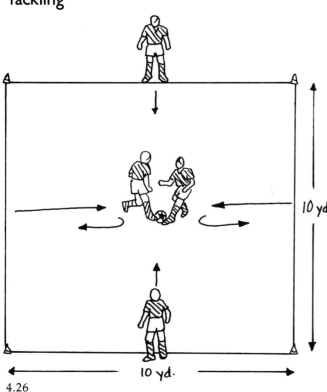

Field Size. 10-yd × 10-yd grid.

Organization. 12 players in groups of four, one soccer ball per group. The four players in each group form a square and place themselves facing a partner. One set of partners jog out simultaneously and tackle for the ball in the middle of the grid (4.26). After the tackle they jog back. The exercise is repeated by the other two players in the group.

4.26

Tackling

4.27

Field Size. 10-yd × 10 yd grid.

Organization. 12 players in groups of four, two soccer balls per group. The four players in each group form a square and place themselves facing a partner with one ball between each pair. One player dribbles the ball out into the center of the grid where the partner tackles for it (4.27). After the tackle both players return to their original positions on the grid and reverse roles. In this exercise the dribbling player does *not* try to dribble past the tackling player.

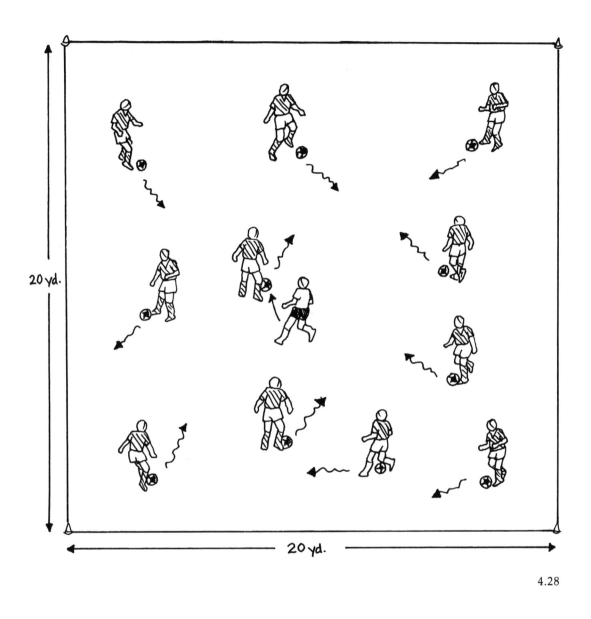

4.28

Field Size 20-yd × 20-yd grid.

Organization: 12 players, 11 soccer balls, four cones. Eleven players each with a ball dribble it around inside the grid; the 12th player attempts to tackle and kick the balls out of the grid (4.28).

Goalkeeping
(Basic Handling—Ground Kneeling Technique)

Organization. Goalkeepers in pairs, with one soccer ball per pair. Place goalkeepers ten yards apart facing each other. Each goalkeeper takes a turn at rolling the ball along the ground one yard to the side of the opposite goalkeeper; the receiver collects it in the kneeling technique and returns the ball in the same manner alternating the sides that the ball is rolled to (4.29).

4.29

Goalkeeping
(Basic Handling—Ground Kneeling Technique—Including Footwork)

Organization. Goalkeepers in pairs, with one soccer ball per pair. Cones are set eight yards apart, forming goals with another two cones positioned one-and-one-half yards inside each post. The goalkeeper should be positioned in the center of the goal before each service. The server stands ten yards away from the goal and rolls the ball alternately to the left and right of the goalkeeper aiming for the cones positioned inside each post (4.30). Goalkeepers must shuttle across to receive the ball in the kneeling technique.

4.30

4.31

Organization. Goalkeepers in pairs with one soccer ball per pair. Cones are set eight yards apart forming goals with another two cones positioned one-and-one-half yards inside each post. The server rolls the ball in between the cone and the post (4.31). Encourage the goalkeeper to shuttle across and collect the ball in the kneeling technique.

Coaching Points

- Head steady, eyes watching the ball.
- Ensure goalkeeper is sideways-on with legs and body behind the ball.
- Ensure that the knee of the kneeling leg is level with the heel of the foot of the other leg.
- Ensure correct knee placement for appropriate side.
- Scoop the ball into the chest.

Goalkeeping
(Basic Handling—Waist Shots)

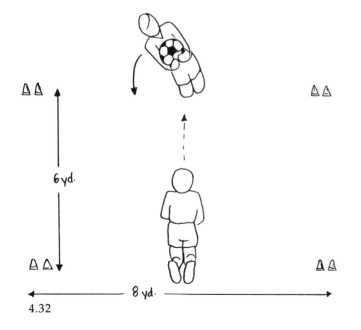

4.32

Field Size. 6-yds × 8-yd grid.

Organization. Goalkeepers in pairs, one soccer ball per pair. Both goalkeepers kneel facing each other. In turn each goalkeeper throws the ball underhand towards the waist of the partner (4.32). Encourage the goalkeepers to reach forward and collect the ball early. If the ball is played to the side the goalkeeper should cup the ball to the body and land on the shoulder—not the elbow.

Goalkeeping
(Basic Handling—Chest Shots)

4.33

Field Size 8-yd × 10-yd grid.

Organization. Goalkeepers in pairs, one soccer ball per pair. In turn each goalkeeper throws the ball overarm towards the chest area of the partner (4.33). Encourage the goalkeeper to step and/or reach forward to collect the ball early. If the ball has been played to the side, the goalkeeper should move sideways and ensure that the body and the arms are behind the ball.

Goalkeeping
(Basic Handling—Waist and Chest Shots)

4.34

Organization. Goalkeepers in pairs, with a number of soccer balls, two cones. Balls are kicked waist- or chest-high to the goalkeeper in the center area of the goal (4.34). Once the goalkeeper shows good technique, the balls should be served towards the cones placed two yards inside each goal post. Encourage the correct sideways movement from the goalkeeper. Goalkeepers change positions every 20 shots.

Coaching Points

- Head steady and eyes on the ball.
- Ensure body and arms are behind the ball on contact.
- Cup the ball into the body for protection.
- If the goalkeeper finds it necessary to dive, land on the shoulder—not on the elbow.

4.35

Organization. Goalkeepers in pairs with a number of soccer balls, four cones. Goalkeeper receives a ball played in by the server, and rolls it underarm through the two cones placed two yards apart and positioned five yards outside each side of the penalty area (4.35). Goalkeepers change positions after 20 throws.

4.36

Organization. Goalkeepers in pairs with a supply of soccer balls, four cones. The goalkeeper in the goal area receives a ball from the server, and throws it javelin style through two cones spaced four yards apart and positioned ten yards from the side of the penalty area (4.36). The goalkeeper should throw from inside the six yard box. The ball may bounce before passing through the cones. Insist on accuracy. Goalkeepers change position every 20 throws.

Goalkeeping
(Distribution—Overarm Throw)

Organization. Goalkeepers in pairs with a supply of soccer balls, four cones. The goalkeeper receives the ball from the server and from the edge of the penalty area throws it overarm through two cones placed 10 yds apart positioned 15 yards from the edge of the penalty area (4.37). Goalkeepers change position every 20 throws.

Goalkeeping
(Shot Stopping—Ground)

Organization. Goalkeepers in pairs, one soccer ball per pair, six cones. The goalkeeper stands one to two yards behind the goal line and does a forward roll as the ball is served *along the ground* one yard to the side, forcing the goalkeeper to dive and save (4.38). The exercise should be repeated on alternate sides. Roles should be reversed every 20 saves.

Organization. Goalkeepers in pairs, one soccer ball per pair, six cones. The goalkeeper stands one to two yards behind the goal line. The server stands six yards out in front of the goal with the ball. The goalkeeper does a forward roll as the server throws the ball underarm *in the air* for the goalkeeper to dive and save (4.39). Roles are reversed every 20 saves.

4.39

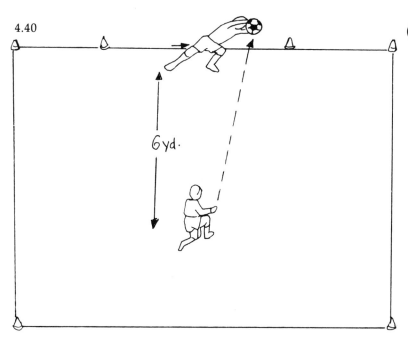

4.40

Organization. Goalkeepers in pairs, six soccer balls, six cones. The goalkeeper stands in the goal. The server rolls the ball along the ground or throws it in the air to the goalkeepers left (4.40). The goalkeeper dives to save it, recovers and returns it to the server who repeats the exercise to the goalkeepers right. Reverse roles every 20 saves.

TEAM GAMES

For all team games: if the ball goes out of play, restart the game with a goal kick or throw-in.

Field Size. 30 yds × 20 yds.

Organization. Three-on-three (4.41). Use cones to make small goals two yards wide.

Attacking	Defending
Depth	Pressure
Width	Cover
Penetration	Balance
1-2's, Support	

4.41

4.42

Field Size. 30 yds × 20 yds.

Organization. Four-on-four (4.42). Use cones to make small goals two yards wide.

Attacking	Defending
Depth	Pressure
Width	Cover
Penetration	Balance
1-2's, Support	

Field Size. 30 yds × 20 yds.

Organization. Four-on-three plus a goalkeeper (4.43). Use cones to make small goals six yards wide. The nearest defending player to the goal must retreat and become the goalkeeper until possession has been won.

Attacking	Defending
Depth	Delay
Width	Pressure
Penetration	Cover
1-2's, Support	Balance

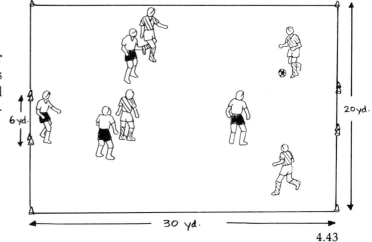

4.43

Field Size. 20-yd × 20-yd grid.

4.44

Organization. Three-on-three, four cones (4.44). Three teams of three. Two teams play against each other. To score a goal a team must knock over a cone with the ball. The teams can play either inside or outside of the cones. The team that scores goes off and the other team comes on.

Attacking
Depth
Width
Penetration
Changing point
of attack
1-2's, Support

Defending
Pressure
Cover
Balance

Organization. Three-on-three with a central goal (4.45). Play three-on-three with a central goal. Both teams can score from either side of the goal. The team that scores goes off and the other team comes on.

Attacking
Depth
Width
Penetration

Defending
Pressure
Cover

4.45

Getting Teams to Spread Out

Organization. One of the most asked questions, is how do you get a young team to spread out and recognize space. There is no easy answer but the series of practices that follow will help. Divide the field into thirds vertically.

Three-on-zero. *No pressure* (4.46). During the course of each practice the attacking players cannot leave their third. The practice starts when the player in the middle third passes the ball into either of the outside thirds. The players continue passing and moving down the field, finishing with a shot on goal. When the shot on goal is completed the next group repeat the exercise.

4.46

Three-on-one. *Increase pressure* (4.47). Add a defender to provide pressure. The defender is free to move from third to third.

4.47

Getting Teams to Spread Out

Three-on-two. *Further increase of pressure* (4.48). Increase the pressure by adding a second defender; same freedom applies.

4.48

Two other methods of getting players to spread out and support are:

Five-on-one. Play five attackers against one defender (4.49). Same restrictions and freedoms apply.

4.49

Getting Teams to Spread Out

Five-on-two. *Increase pressure* (4.50). Increase
the pressure by adding a second defender; same
freedom applies.

4.50

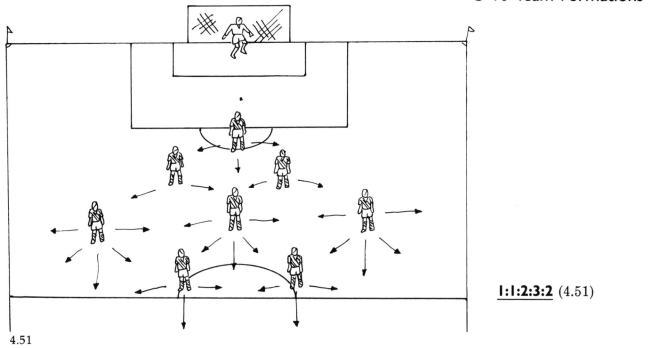

1:1:2:3:2 (4.51)

4.51

1:3:3:2 (4.52)

4.52

U-10 Team Formations

1:2:4:2 (4.53)

4.53

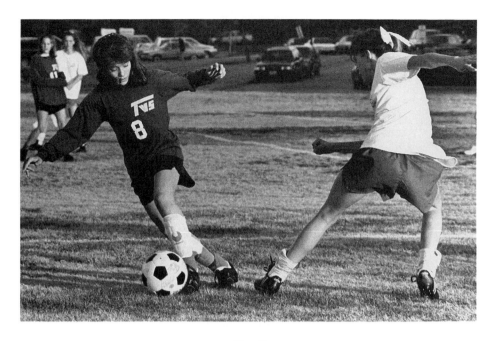

V

U-12 DRILLS & PRACTICES

(under age 12)

At this age level small-sided games are still your primary focus for team play, but you also want to concentrate on individual ball work, juggling, running with the ball, etc. Instruct your players to work in two's and three's, stressing that the emphasis of the exercise is on cooperation.

Length of Training Session: 90 Minutes

- **Warm-up.** 10 minutes

- **Technique/Skill Development.** 20 minutes

- **Team Games/Set Plays.** 40 minutes

- **Free Play.** 20 minutes

Warm-up

5.1

Organization. Players in groups of five. The players move around the whole time while playing the ball performing 1-2's (wall pass) and takeovers (crossover runs) (5.1). Make sure the players use the whole of the area.

Warm-up

5.2

Field Size. 20-yd × 20-yd grid.

Organization. Five-on-two, one soccer ball, four cones. Play five-on-two in the whole of the grid area for two minutes, then change defenders (5.2).

5.3

Field Size. Half a field.

Organization. Players in groups of five, one soccer ball per group. Using the instep, the player with the ball plays it to the farthest player in the group. This player lays it off to one of the supporting players (5.3). The receiving player controls, dribbles and repeats the exercise.

Dribbling—Shielding

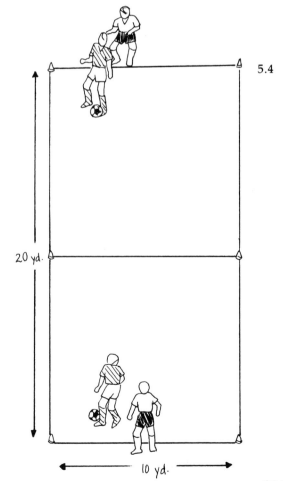

5.4

20 yd.

10 yd.

Field Size. 20-yd × 10-yd grid.

Organization. Players in pairs, one soccer ball per pair, six cones. The player with the ball should dribble and shield it, attempting to reach either of the corner cones (5.4). If successful a point is awarded. Once the player with the ball has had one touch the opponent can enter the grid to prevent a point being scored. The opponent gets a point for winning the ball.

Dribbling—Shielding

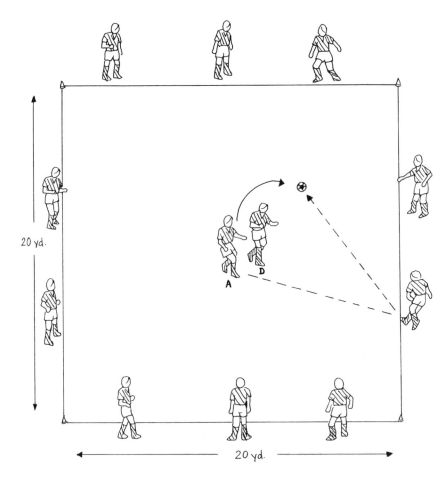

5.5

Field Size. 20-yd × 20-yd grid.

Organization. 12 players, one soccer ball, four cones. Ten players are situated on the outside of the grid. The other two on the inside play one-on-one, using the players on the outside for passing situations, using one and two touches (5.5). The aim is to get possession of the ball by passing and shielding and trying to get behind the defender.

Dribbling—Turning

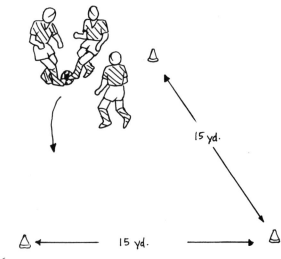

5.6

Field Size. 15-yd × 15-yd grid.

Organization. One-on-one-on-one, one soccer ball, three cones. Each player attempts to gain possession of the ball (5.6). When possession is gained, the player must try to score a goal by knocking down one of the cones.

5.7

Field Size. 10-yd × 10-yd grids.

Organization. The defending players are situated on the far line of each grid and can only challenge for the ball when the attacking players enter their grid (5.7).

The attacking players commence the practice by attempting to dribble the ball through each grid, past the defender until they reach the other end or lose it to a defender (5.8). The ball is then dribbled back to the start on the outside of the grids.

5.8

107

Kicking—Inside of the Foot—Passing

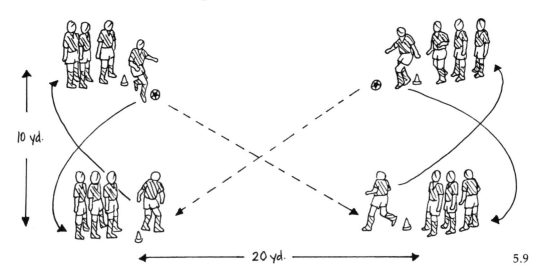

5.9

Field Size. 20-yd × 10-yd grid.

Organization. Four groups of four, two soccer balls, four cones. Each player in turn plays the ball to the player diagonally opposite, then runs to the back of the group alongside (5.9).

Kicking—Inside of the Foot—Passing

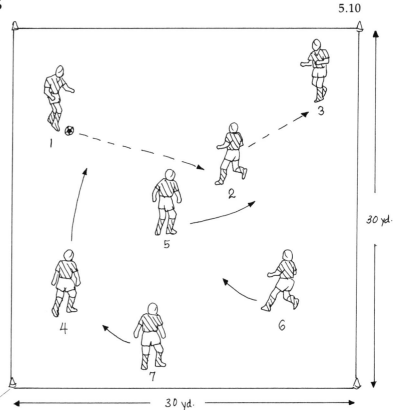

5.10

Field Size. 30-yd × 30-yd grid.

Organization. Players numbered 1 to 7. Players move around inside grid while passing the ball in numerical order using the inside of the foot (5.10).

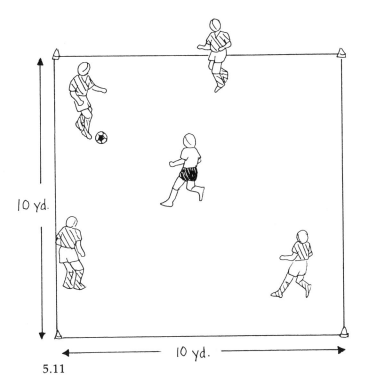

10 yd.

10 yd.

5.11

Field Size. 10-yd × 10-yd grid.

Organization. Five players, one soccer ball, four cones. Play four-on-one; first pass is free. The four players towards the outside of the grid use one and two touches and try to keep the ball away from the defender in the middle of the grid (5.11). If a player near the outside misses the ball, that player becomes the defender—or the coach can set a time limit.

Kicking—Inside of the Foot—Passing

Field Size. 30 yds long.

Organization. Four players per group, one soccer ball per group, two cones per group. To start the practice, using the inside of the foot, the end player plays the ball to the third player who passes it using one touch to the second player, who also uses one touch to pass it to the fourth player (5.12). This player has two touches; one to control the ball and the other to repeat the exercise. The coach can make this exercise into a competitive game by playing the groups against each other.

5.12

Kicking—Inside of the Foot—Passing

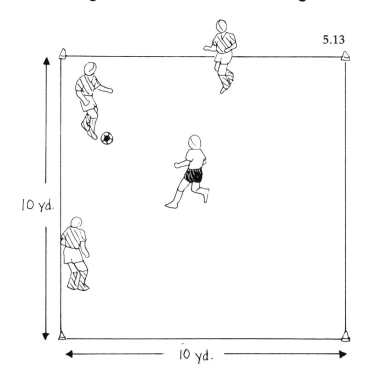

5.13

Field Size. 10-yd × 10-yd grid.

Organization. Three-on-one. The three players towards the outside of the grid pass and move into open spaces to achieve maximum time and space. They try to keep the ball away from the defender in the middle of the grid (5.13). If a player near the outside misses the ball, that player becomes the defender—or the coach can set a time limit. This practice should help players understand *short support.*

Kicking—Inside of the Foot—Passing

5.14

Field Size. 20-yd × 20-yd grid.

Organization. Four-on-two. The four players on the outside of the grid pass and move into open spaces to achieve maximum time and space. They try to keep the ball away from the two defenders in the middle of the grid (5.14). If a player on the outside misses the ball, that player becomes the defender—or the coach can set a time limit. This practice should help players understand *short and long support* and *penetration* (splitting the two defenders).

110

Field Size. Half a field.

Organization. Split the team into groups A and B with one target player on the edge of the penalty box, and a goalkeeper in goal. A player from group A commences the practice by chipping a long pass to the target player who lays the ball off to a player from group B who is running forwards to shoot on goal (5.15). After each shot the players should rotate clockwise.

Coaching Points

- Stress accurate chipping.
- Lay the ball off with one touch.
- Hitting the goal.

5.15

Kicking—Volleys—Shooting

Field Size. 10-yd $\times$ 10-yd grid in the attacking third of the field.

Organization. Players in pairs, one soccer ball per pair, four cones. One player from each pair stands behind the 10-yard $\times$ 10-yard grid facing the goal. The partner stands behind the goal line with a ball (5.16). The player with the ball punts it from the hands to a partner who controls the ball out of the air, or following one bounce inside the grid, using one of the six controlling surfaces. The player with the ball then takes a shot on goal. After each attempt these players go to the back of the opposite group. The coach can make this exercise into a competitive game by playing two-on-two.

5.16

Kicking—Lofted Passing

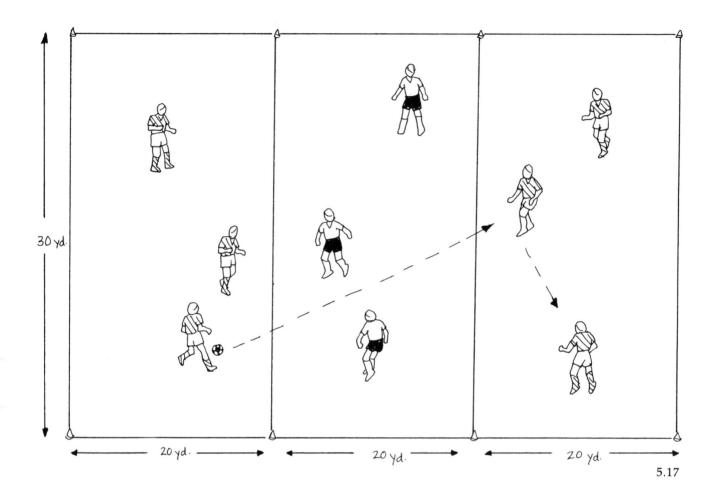

30 yd.

20 yd.   20 yd.   20 yd.

5.17

Field Size. 30-yd × 20-yd grids.

Organization. Nine players, one soccer ball, eight cones. Split the grid size into three equal areas with three players in each. The players at each end pass the ball to one another and to the players at the far end. The players in the middle area try to anticipate and intercept the passes (5.17). Limit the players at each end to two touches and only three passes. Points are scored for a good pass from one end to the other, and the players in the middle get a point if a pass is intercepted and controlled.

Coaching Points

- Look for through passes that split defenders.
- Receivers must move to establish good passing angles.
- Communication is very important.

Field Size.
Attacking third of the field.

Organization. Players in five groups, a number of soccer balls, four cones. Two groups are positioned each side of the field with the balls. These players carry the ball down the touch line to make a cross into the near or far post area (5.18). The two groups on the outside of the center group—all positioned outside of the penalty box—make runs to the near and far post areas to shoot on goal. A player from the center group acts as a trailer.

5.18

Kicking—Lofted Passing—Crossing

5.19

Field Size.
Attacking third of the field.

Organization. Players in six groups, a number of soccer balls, six cones. The ball is played from a wide midfield player to a player situated outside the field (5.19). This player plays the ball back to the midfielder who plays it into space (a double pass) for the wide player to run onto and cross either to the far or near post areas. The players from the groups situated in the center can either make a bent or cross-over run to the post areas and shoot on goal. The same exercise is conducted by the players on the other side of the field.

Kicking—Lofted Passing—Crossing

5.20

Field Size. Full field.

Organization. Players in six groups, two goal-keepers, a number of soccer balls, two cones. The coach is positioned in the center circle with the soccer balls and plays a ball out to a wide player who carries it down the touch line and crosses it to the near post area (5.20). The group positioned on the edge of the penalty box runs to that area while the group positioned wide on that side runs to the far post area in an attempt on goal. The exercise is repeated at the opposite end of the field.

5.21

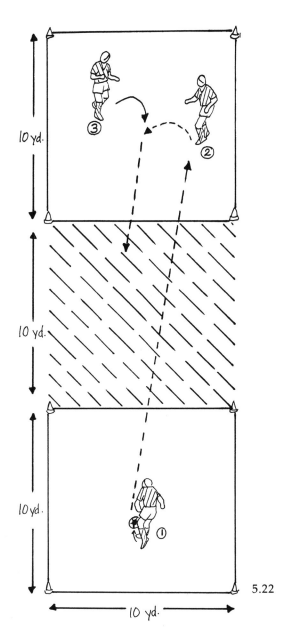

5.22

Field Size. 30 yds long.

Organization. Players in groups of four, one soccer ball and two cones per group. Make sure that the players at each end stay behind the line. One of the end players commences the practice by passing the ball to the next player in line; this player must come to meet the ball, turn and with one touch pass it to the next player in line (5.21). This is repeated until the ball reaches the player at the far end who has two touches; one to control and the other to pass back and repeat the exercise.

Field Size. 30-yd × 10-yd grids.

Organization. Three players and one soccer ball per group, eight cones. The player at one end of the grid chips the ball to one of the other players at the other end of the grid (5.22). The receiver controls the ball inside the grid and then passes it to the partner who chips it back to the server. The server in turn controls it and returns it to a player in the far grid. Continue the exercise.

Aerial Control

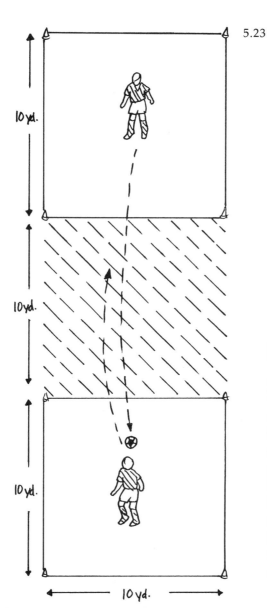

10 yd.

10 yd.

10 yd.

10 yd.

Field Size. 30-yd × 10-yd grids.

Organization. Players in pairs with one soccer ball per pair, eight cones. The ball is played to a partner to control and chip back (5.23). The exercise should be repeated trapping the ball, using all of the six body surfaces (5.24). The body must be in line with the ball and an early decision must be made as to the surface to use. The ball must be caught for a point after controlling it with one of the six body surfaces.

5.24

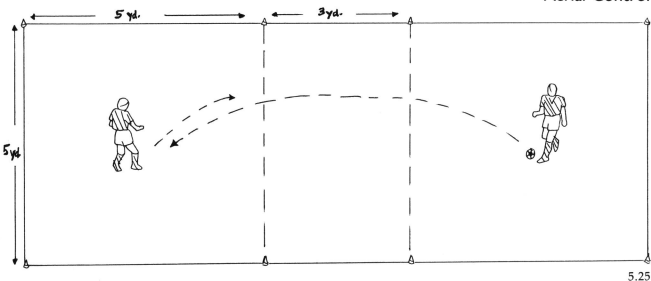

5.25

Field Size. 13-yd × 5-yd grid.

Organization. Players in pairs, one soccer ball per pair, eight cones. The first player punts the ball from inside the grid to a player in the opposite end of the grid who controls it using one of the six controlling surfaces, either out of the air, or allowing only one bounce on the ground (5.25). The ball is then played back and the exercise repeated.

Step 1

Step 2

5.26   Step 3

Organization. Players in pairs, one soccer ball per pair. The players stand opposite one another, 10 yards apart (5.26). The practice starts with one player taking a proper throw-in to the receiving partner who must control the ball out of the air using one of the six controlling surfaces, then play it back on the second touch.

Progression. When the ball is returned to the thrower, it must be controlled out of the air and caught for a point.

117

Aerial Control

Field Size. 40-yd × 20-yd grid.

Organization. 10 players, two teams of five, one soccer ball per team, 15 cones. Team members place themselves one in each grid and one outside at the end (5.27). The outside player punts the ball to the player in the first grid who must control, turn, and gently volley the ball to the player in the next part of the grid. This is repeated until the ball reaches the player in the last section of the grid who controls and catches it for a point. If the ball hits the ground or a team member leaves a grid, the team must start over.

Progression. Two touch, three touch—using only the designated body surfaces.

5.27

Aerial Control

5.28

Field Size. Attacking third of field.

Organization. Players in pairs, one soccer ball per pair. The first two players of each group commence the practice when one player bounces the ball, then kicks it in the air to a partner (5.28). The partner allows it to bounce then controls it using one of the six controlling surfaces. Following another bounce it is played to the partner who has run past. The exercise is repeated until either partner can take a shot on goal. We recommend that a goalkeeper not be used. The ball must hit the goal net on the full (fly) to score. If either of the partners makes a mistake on the way to goal they return to the back of the group and the exercise is repeated by the next two players in line.

5.29

Organization. Players in groups of four, one soccer ball per group. The first player bounces the ball then passes it in the air to the next player who must control, using the chest and thigh, before turning and passing it on (5.29). This pattern is repeated backwards and forwards along the line of players.

Heading—Attacking

5.30

Field Size. The center circle.

Organization. Players in pairs, one soccer ball per pair, 10 cones. Players form a circle facing a partner. Ten cones are placed in the middle of the circle. One player chips the ball over the cones to a partner who must head the ball in an attempt to knock over the cones (5.30). Change roles every 10 tries.

Heading—Defending

5.31

Organization. Players in two groups, one soccer ball, two cones. Two cones are placed ten yards apart with a group of players at each cone. The practice starts with the first player serving the ball underhand to the front player of the group opposite then running to the back of that group (5.31). The receiving player heads the ball back to the next player of the opposite group then runs to the back of that group. The exercise is repeated with the remaining players heading the ball back and forth and running to the end of the opposite group. If the ball hits the ground the exercise is restarted from the beginning.

Heading—Passing

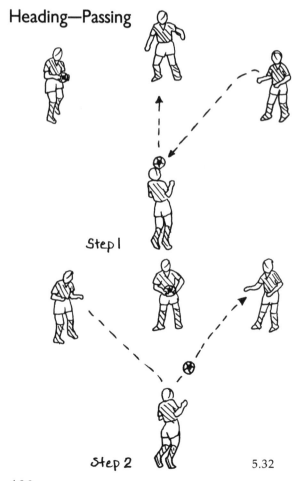

Step 1

Step 2

5.32

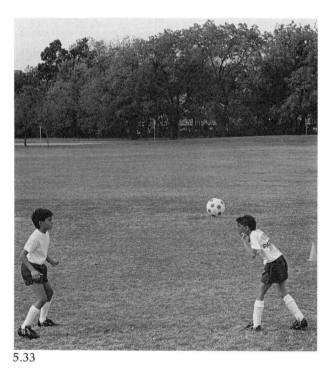

5.33

Organization. Four players, two soccer balls. Step 1: one of the players with a ball throws it underhand to the receiving player who heads to the player without a ball (5.32). Step 2: the other player with the ball repeats the exercise and play continues (5.33).

120

5.34

Field Size. 10-yd × 10-yd grid.

Organization. Two players and a goalkeeper, two soccer balls, four cones. Position the goalkeeper in the middle of the grid facing the first server. The ball is thrown underhand at varying heights to the goalkeeper who gathers and returns it to the first server before spinning round to receive the next ball thrown by the second server (5.34).

Goalkeeping
(Basic Handling)

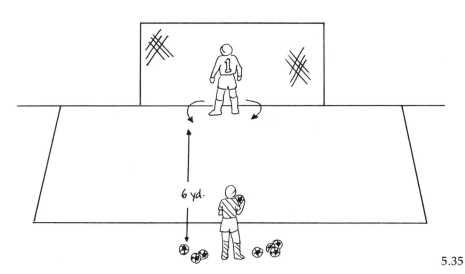

5.35

Organization. Goalkeeper, one player, a number of soccer balls. The goalkeeper stands in the middle of the goal on the goal line facing away from the server who stands six yards from the goalkeeper (5.35). The server calls the side that the ball is to be served to and the goalkeeper must react by turning and saving it.

Goalkeeping
(Basic Handling)

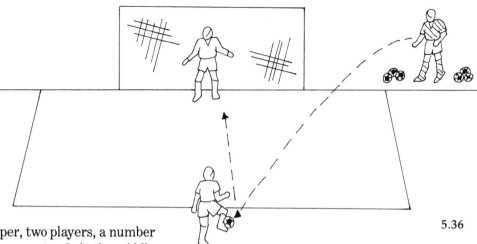

5.36

Organization. Goalkeeper, two players, a number of soccer balls. The goalkeeper stands in the middle of the goal on the goal line. One player stands on the goal line with the balls, near the edge of the six yard box, and throws a ball underhand in the air to the other player standing six yards out from the center of the goal (5.36). The ball is *gently* volleyed, using the inside of the foot to the goalkeeper who makes a save and returns it to the server. The exercise is repeated. Ensure that the shots played to the goalkeeper are not struck too hard. As in all practices adjust to the goalkeeper's abilities.

Coaching Points

- Correct starting position.
- Head steady and eyes on the ball.
- Ensure the correct technique is applied depending on reaction.
- Good feet movement if necessary.

Goalkeeping
(Shot Stopping)

5.37

Organization. Goalkeeper, one player, a number of soccer balls. The goalkeeper stands in the center of the goal on the goal line. The other player stands six to eight yards out in front of the goal with a supply of balls (5.37). Using the inside of the foot, the player serves a ball along the ground one yard to the side of the goalkeeper who drops to save it. The exercise is repeated to the goalkeeper's opposite side.

5.38

Organization. Goalkeeper, two players, one soccer ball. The goalkeeper positions himself on the knees six yards from the server who throws the ball above the goalkeepers head (5.38). The goalkeeper, using both hands, should palm it over an imaginary crossbar. The second player catches and returns it to the server.

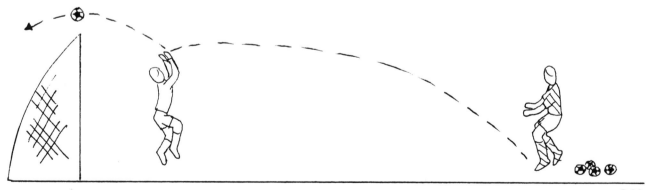

5.39

Organization. Goalkeeper, one player, a number of soccer balls. The goalkeeper stands in the middle of the goal on the goal line. As the goalkeeper advances forward towards the six-yard line, the server volleys a ball just above the goalkeeper's head (5.39). The goalkeeper should flex the knees, angle back, and deflect the ball over the crossbar using both hands.

Goalkeeping
(Distribution—Goal Kick)

5.40

Organization. Two players, goalkeeper with a number of soccer balls, four cones. The goalkeeper takes a dead-ball kick (goal kick) and attempts to play the ball through two cones spaced 10 yards apart and 25 yards from the goal line. The ball must pass through the cones on the full (5.40). Attempt 10 goal kicks from each side of the goal. As efficiency improves, increase the distance accordingly.

5.41

Organization. Goalkeeper, one player with a number of soccer balls, six cones. The serving player plays the ball to the goalkeeper who collects it on the edge of the penalty area and distributes it, using either a punt or an overarm throw through any of three sets of cones (5.41). Each set of cones is positioned across the pitch, 15 yards apart and 40 yards out from the goal line. The ball may bounce prior to going through the cones.

Goalkeeping
(Distribution)

5.42

Organization. Goalkeeper, one player with a number of soccer balls, 14 cones. The goalkeeper receives a ball played in by the serving player and distributes it through any of the sets of cones (5.42). The goalkeeper should use a punt (volley), a dropkick (half-volley), or a throw (overarm, javelin, underarm). Vary the serve so that the goalkeeper can use all of the techniques required for good distribution. The ball may contact the ground prior to passing through the cones.

5.43

Organization. Goalkeeper, one player with a number of soccer balls. The serving player stands at one side and on the edge of the six-yard area.

The server throws a ball gently to the goalkeeper who collects it in the air, pulls it down into the chest, and then returns it to the server (5.43). Encourage the goalkeeper to attack the ball down a route which allows the earliest possible contact. After 10 serves change sides.

12 yd.

5.44

Organization. Goalkeeper, two or three players with a number of soccer balls. The two serving players are positioned one on each side of the penalty area and 12 yards out from the goal line.

Position the goalkeeper in the six-yard box. Each server in turn throws the ball overarm for the goalkeeper to collect (5.44). If the goalkeeper shows confidence when collecting the crosses, add a passive opponent in the six-yard box. Encourage the goalkeeper to call "keepers" when collecting the crosses.

Goalkeeping
(Crosses—Catching—Punching)

Organization. Goalkeeper, four players, two with a number of soccer balls. Position the goalkeeper in the goal with two other players, one as an opponent and the other as a teammate. The other two players should be positioned as servers just inside the penalty box (5.45).

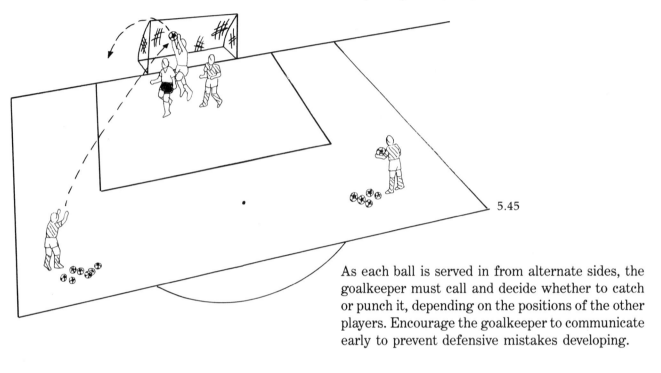

5.45

As each ball is served in from alternate sides, the goalkeeper must call and decide whether to catch or punch it, depending on the positions of the other players. Encourage the goalkeeper to communicate early to prevent defensive mistakes developing.

Goalkeeping
(Narrowing the Angle)

5.46

Organization. Goalkeeper, three players, each with a soccer ball. Position the three players around the penalty area (5.46). On the command from the coach the goalkeeper advances towards the nominated player and attempts to narrow the angle and to make the save before recovering to repeat the exercise.

5.47

Organization. One player and a goalkeeper with a number of soccer balls. The goalkeeper who is positioned in the goal serves the ball out to the player on the edge of the penalty box who is limited to 2 touches (5.47). As the player plays the ball at varying angles with the first touch, the goalkeeper readjusts position and narrows the angle to receive the shot.

Goalkeeping
(Narrowing the Angle)

5.48

Organization. Goalkeeper, three players, one with a number of soccer balls. Position the goalkeeper in the middle of the six-yard box. The server, stationed to one side of the goal, plays the ball out to either of the players on the edge of the penalty area inside the "D." The players can pass back and forth, dribble in on the goalkeeper, or shoot (5.48). The goalkeeper must decide whether to advance and/or readjust sideways to narrow the angle and make the save. The goalkeeper must reposition after the shot is made to repeat the exercise.

5.49

Field Size. 30 yds $\times$ 20 yds.

Organization. Three-on-two and two-on-three grid game. To score the attacking players must dribble or pass the ball through the small goals (5.49). If a defending player wins the ball, it must be passed quickly to an attacking partner in the other half of the grid. When a goal is scored the ball goes to a defender for a free pass. Change roles every five goals.

5.50

Field Size. 50 yds $\times$ 45 yds.

Organization. Four-on-four plus goalkeepers, two wide neutral players. The wide players must stay in their zone but can be used by the team in possession of the ball to advance down the field (5.50).

Progression. Play three-on-three plus goalkeepers but add another two wide players with the restriction that they can only receive the ball in their half of the field (5.51). After a challenge they must get back quickly.

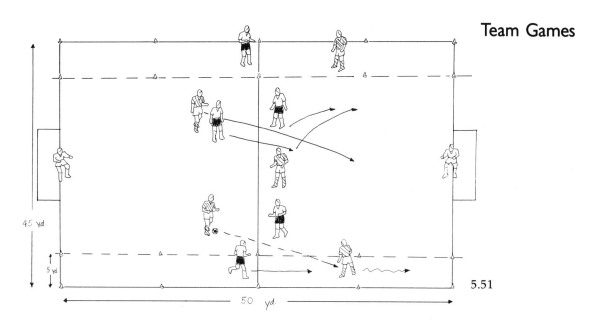

5.51

Keep Away

Team Games—Keep Away

Field Size. 60 yds × 40 yds.

Organization. Team players, one soccer ball, four cones. Play the keep-away games (5.52) in combinations of six-on-four, five-on-five, six-on-six, seven-on-seven.

5.52

5.53

Field Size. Half of the field.

Organization. Six-on-six. To score a point the team in possession must dribble the ball over the half way line or goal line (5.53).

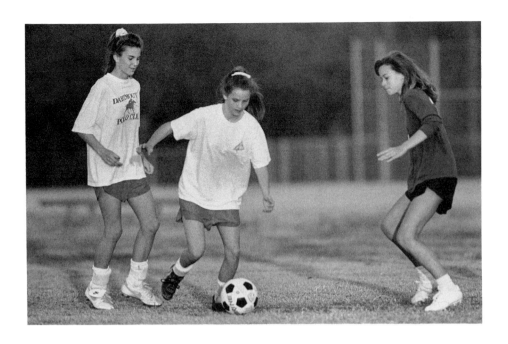

VI

U-15 DRILLS & PRACTICES

(under age 15)

At this age level your emphasis shifts from small-sided games to a concentration on small group practices—five-on-five through to seven-on-seven. The focus of these group practices converges on team formations and shape.

Length of Training Session: 90 Minutes

- **Warm-up.** 10 minutes

- **Technique/Skill Development.** 20 minutes

- **Team Games/Set Plays.** 40 minutes

- **Free Play.** 20 minutes

PRACTICES

Warm-up

Step 1   Step 2   Step 3   6.1

Organization. Players in pairs, one soccer ball per pair. One player sits down while the other juggles the ball. The coach nominates one of the six controlling surfaces. The juggling player kicks the ball up in the air for the sitting player to rise and control with the nominated surface (6.1). Repeat exercise alternating roles.

6.2

Field Size. 15-yd × 15-yd grids.

Organization. Two groups with players numbered 1–7 in each, one soccer ball per group, eight cones. Commence the practice with each team in their own grid passing the ball freely. The coach nominates two players by number to enter the opponents grid and attempt to win the ball during a period of two minutes (6.2). Then another two players are nominated and the first two return to their grid. The exercise is repeated and the score is kept by counting the number of successful passes and intercepts.

133

Dribbling

6.3

Field Size.
Attacking third of field.

Field Size.
Attacking third of field.

Organization. Players in groups of six, one server with a number of soccer balls, one goalkeeper, two cones. The server plays the ball over the goal. One player from each group runs forward to challenge for it (6.3). The player that wins the ball first becomes the attacker and the other the defender. The attacker attempts to beat the defender and score a goal. The coach should encourage players to control the ball quickly, shield properly, and shoot when an opportunity arises.

Dribbling

Field Size. Half of the field.

Organization. Four groups of players plus a goalkeeper, a number of soccer balls, four cones. The two groups on the goal line have the soccer balls. A ball is driven *along the ground* towards a player on the halfway line (6.4). The receiving player runs forward, controls, and dribbles the ball towards goal attempting to beat the server by dribbling around this opponent, finishing with a shot on goal. Following each attempt the players go to the back of the opposite group.

Progression. Play the ball *in the air* to the receiver.

6.4

Dribbling

Field Size.
Half of the field.

Organization. Two groups of players plus two goalkeepers, a number of soccer balls. Two portable goals are placed on the edge of the penalty box. The defending players stand between the goals. The group of attacking players are positioned in the center circle with the soccer balls. The attacker dribbles the ball forward and attempts to beat the defender, and then have a shot on either goal (6.5).

Progression. The defender passes the ball to the attacker, then quickly follows up to challenge.

6.5

25 yd.

25 yd.

44 yd.

6.6

Dribbling

Field Size. 50 yds × 44 yds.

Organization. One-on-one plus a goalkeeper in each half of the area, one soccer ball, six cones. The player with the ball passes it to an attacking team player in the other half of the area. The attacker controls and attempts to dribble around the opponent and score (6.6). If the opponent wins the ball, it should be played back to the other end for a quick counterattack.

Kicking—Shooting

Field Size. Penalty box.

Organization. Set up cones 16 yards from the goal and six yards apart. The shooting player dribbles to the cone, performs a fake, beats the cone to the outside, and finishes with a shot on goal (6.7).

Variations. Attack the cone to the inside. Attack the cone from either side. Dribble diagonally to the far cone.

6.7

Kicking—Shooting

6.8

Field Size. Penalty box.

Organization. Groups of three plus a goalkeeper, a number of soccer balls, four cones placed 10 yards by 10 yards apart in the center of the penalty box. The serving players alternately serve balls on the ground or in the air to the shooting player (6.8). Restrict the shooter to two touches. Emphasize concentration and hitting the target.

Kicking—Shooting

Field Size. Penalty box.

Organization. Two groups of eight plus a goalkeeper, a number of soccer balls. The coach serves a ball from the edge of the "D" into the penalty box (6.9). The player that wins the ball can either shoot or pass to another teammate for a shot on goal.

Progression. The players must make three passes before taking a shot. Players must make a wall pass before taking a shot.

6.9

6.10

Field Size. Penalty box.

Organization. Players in pairs, a number of soccer balls. The two players in the penalty box play together as a partnership; one player will be the target and the other will shoot (6.10). After one minute they change roles. The players on the outside alternate playing ground or air balls into the target player who lays it off for the shooter to shoot first time. After two minutes change partnership.

Kicking—Volleys

6.11

Field Size. Attacking third of field

Organization. Five players plus a goalkeeper, a number of soccer balls, four cones set out in a 10-yard by 10-yard grid in the penalty box. Four servers are numbered 1–4, each with a supply of soccer balls. The coach calls a number and the player in the grid looks towards that server to receive the pass, control then volley the ball towards goal (6.11). Restrict the shooter to two touches. Emphasize concentration and hitting the target.

Kicking—Volleys

6.12

Field Size. 44 yds × 36 yds.

Organization. Five players plus two goalkeepers, a number of soccer balls, four cones set out in a 10-yard by 10-yard grid in the center of the playing area. Four servers are numbered 1–4, each with a supply of soccer balls. The coach calls a number and the player in the grid looks towards that server to receive the pass, control then volley the ball towards either goal (6.12). Emphasize concentration and hitting the target.

Progression

- The shooter must shoot towards the goal from the same end that the service came from.
- The shooter must shoot towards the goal on the opposite end from where the service came.
- The shooter must shoot on the second touch with a bounce.
- The shooter must shoot on the second touch without a bounce.
- The shooter must shoot first time.

Passing—Control

6.13

Field Size.
50-yd × 10-yd grid.

Organization. Groups of five, one soccer ball per group, eight cones. The end player chips the ball to player 3; this player plays the ball back along the ground to player 2 (6.13). Player 2 passes it along the ground to player 4 who plays it back to player 3. Player 3 then plays it to player 5 who lofts the ball back to the first player. All ground passes should be one touch except for the end players who have two touches.

Field Size. Half of the field.

Organization. 11 players plus a goal-keeper. The ball is served to a defender, who plays it back. The server plays the ball into space behind the defender to a wide player. The wide player then runs to the far post. The defender turns, tracks down the wide player and applies pressure to the cross. The other wide player runs to the near post (6.14). The coach can also have the server make a run to the near post with the other wide player making a run to the far post.

6.14

6.15

Field Size. Half of the field.

Organization. Two groups of players plus two goalkeepers, a number of soccer balls. A serving player chips the ball to the near goalkeeper then makes a run down the line; the goalkeeper collects the ball, then redistributes it back to the server.

The server controls and crosses either to the near or far post to a player from the opposite group who has run forward to shoot on goal (6.15). The exercise is repeated and the goalkeepers are changed after each goal.

Progression. Change teams over.

Passing—Crosses

6.16

Field Size. Full field.

Organization. Two groups of players plus two goalkeepers, a number of soccer balls. The coach is positioned in the center circle with the soccer balls, and two strikers are positioned in each penalty box. The coach serves a ball out to a wide player who controls it and moves forward down the touch line (6.16). Once close to the goal line the player with the ball makes a 360 degree turn to represent a challenge or problem. Now the runners to the near or far post will have to make changes to their runs. The near post runner should turn away and reopen the near post space to allow the far post runner to run into, then loop towards, the far post. The new near post runner must attack the space at speed as the ball is crossed into the penalty area.

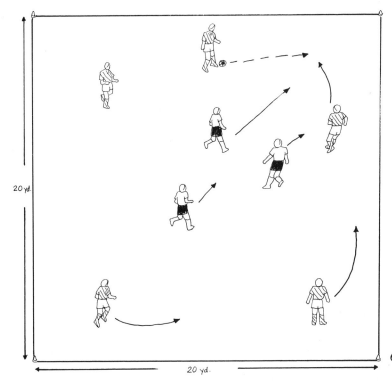

Field Size. 20-yd × 20-yd grid.

Organization. Eight players, one soccer ball, four cones. Five players with the ball attempt to keep it away from the other three (6.17). Any attacking player who makes a mistake or gives the ball away changes places with the defender who has been in the longest. Or the coach can select to play a time-limited game of two minutes.

6.17

Passing—Lofted

Field Size. 30-yd × 10-yd grid.

Organization. Players in pairs, one soccer ball per pair, eight cones. Playing two-on-two, commence the practice with a player passing the ball in the air across the middle grid to a player in the far grid who must control and lay it off for a partner to play it back across (6.18). Repeat the exercise.

Passing—Control

Field Size. 30-yd × 10-yd grid.

Organization. Eight players, one soccer ball, eight cones. Play the ball across the dead space into the opposite grid. Once under control the three attackers must keep the ball away from the lone defender and set up a pass back across to the opposite grid (6.19). If the defender wins the ball, the player that makes the mistake changes places.

6.19

6.18

Passing

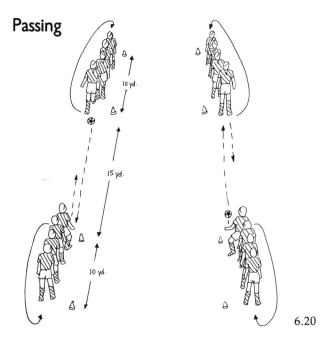

6.20

Field Size. 35-yd × 10-yd grid.

Organization. Four groups, two soccer balls, eight cones. The player with the ball passes it using the inside of the foot to the front player of the group opposite, then moves to the back of the team (6.20). The receiving player repeats the exercise.

6.21

Field Size. 35-yd × 10-yd grid.

Organization. Four groups, two soccer balls, eight cones. The player with the ball passes it diagonally using the inside of the foot to the front player of the group diagonally opposite, then moves around the end cone to the back of that group (6.21). The receiving player repeats the exercise.

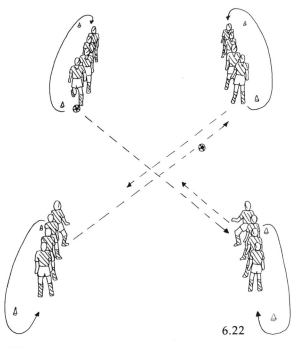

6.22

Passing

Field Size. 35-yd × 10-yd grid.

Organization. Four groups, two soccer balls, eight cones. The player with the ball passes it diagonally using the inside of the foot to the front player of the group diagonally opposite, then moves to the back of his own group (6.22). The receiving player repeats the exercise.

Field Size.
30-yd × 30-yd grid.

Organization. Eight players inside the grid, each with a soccer ball, eight players outside the grid, four cones. The players inside the grid dribble and pass the ball performing wall passes and overlaps with the outside players (6.23). After a time frame reverse the roles.

6.23

Passing—Control

Field Size. 20-yd × 20 yd grid.

Organization. Four groups, two soccer balls, four cones. The player from the first group with the ball passes it forward and follows the pass, moving to the back of the receiving group. The receiving player controls the ball, turns, then passes it (6.24). The exercise is repeated. Encourage players to use either foot by reversing the direction of the practice.

6.24

Passing—Control

Field Size.
80-yd × 40-yd grid. 6.25

Organization. Two groups numbered 1–7, two soccer balls, six cones. Each team must pass and control the ball in numerical order within their 40-yard by 40-yard grid (6.25).

Progression. Remove the midline and allow both groups to play in the 80-yard by 40-yard area (6.26). This will provide unopposed obstruction and players will have to deal with the opening and closing of space.

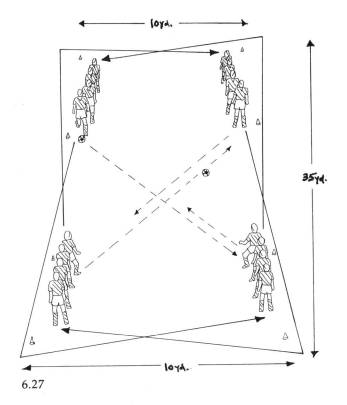

6.27

Field Size. 35-yd × 10-yd grids.

Organization. Four groups, two soccer balls, eight cones. The player plays the ball diagonally using the inside of the foot, then runs around the back to the back of team diagonally opposite (6.27).

6.28

Progression

- The attacker, with one touch, passes the ball to a partner to control and catch.
- The attacker, with one touch, passes the ball to a partner to shoot first time at goal.
- The attacker controls, turns, and shoots at goal with a two-touch total.

Field Size. 70-yd × 40-yd grid.

Organization. 10 players, one soccer ball, eight cones. Play three-on-three in the middle third. Each team has two target players in their attacking third. The players in the middle should attempt to create space allowing a pass in the air to one of their target players (6.28). The player must control the ball and catch it for a point. The target players are free to move anywhere inside their third of the field.

Passing—Inside of the Foot

Field Size. 40-yd × 40-yd grid.

Organization. 14 players, one soccer ball, four cones. Four players from each team are positioned on the outside of the grid, and three players from each team on the inside. Playing three-on-three inside the grid, the players in possession of the ball can also use the outside team players if necessary to maintain possession (6.29). The players outside the grid can only use one touch to pass the ball back.

Progression. When an outside player is in possession of the ball, the opposition player may apply pressure.

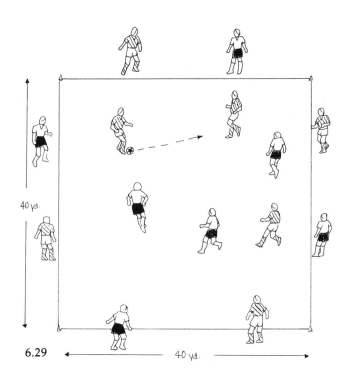

Coaching Points

- Possession.
- Support angles.
- Support distance.
- Short and long support.

Aerial Control

Field Size. 40-yd × 10-yd grid.

Organization. Players in groups of four, one soccer ball per group. The groups of players are positioned in a straight line. The first player throws the ball to the second player who controls it on the chest and lays it back at an angle to the first player, who then chips the ball to the distant fourth player to catch (6.30). Step 2 is to repeat the exercise in reverse. The coach can make a competitive game by playing the groups against each other.

Field Size. 44 yds × 36 yds.

Organization. Players in numbered pairs, two goalkeepers, one soccer ball per pair.

- One player dribbles the ball while the partner moves around (6.31). When the coach nominates a controlling surface the ball is stopped then played in the air to the partner who controls it with that surface, as shown in 1, 3, 5, and 6. The controlling player dribbles the ball away.
- As a variation to the basic exercise, when the coach calls a number and the controlling surface to be used, the players advance to the goal area. The ball is played as in the first exercise ending with a shot on goal as shown in 2 and 4.
- Double the number of partners, then have them go to either goal using 1–2's and combination plays finishing with a shot.

6.31

Aerial Control

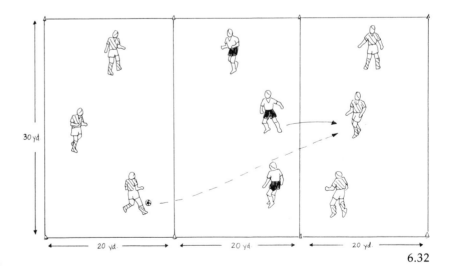

6.32

Field Size. 60-yd × 30-yd grid.

Organization. Nine players, one soccer ball, eight cones, three players per grid. The ball should be played in the air across the middle of the grid to the opposite end of the grid. Once controlled the players must keep possession from a defender who has entered the grid (6.32). The ball should then be returned in the same manner to the opposite end, and the defender returns to the middle. Another defender applies pressure at the opposite end.

Heading

6.33

Field Size. Penalty box.

Organization. Six players, one goalkeeper, a number of soccer balls. Four players, with the soccer balls, take turns at serving them one at a time to the two attacking players to head in an attempt to score (6.33).

Heading

Field Size. 60 yds × 40 yds.

Organization. 12 players, two goalkeepers, one soccer ball, four cones. Practice commences with a player throwing the ball in the air to a teammate who heads to another member of the team who catches it (6.34). The sequence is: throw, head, catch. Any interception by the opposing players must be done in this sequence. A goal can only be scored when the ball is headed.

6.35

Progression

- Add one more defender.
- Add two more defenders.
- Add a third attacker.
- Add a third defender.

Coaching Points

- Head the ball into the goal in the direction that it came from.
- Head the ball down and away from the goalkeeper.
- Head the ball back across the face of the goal if a direct header cannot be taken.

6.34

Heading

Field Size. Full width × 40 yds.

Organization. 10 players, two goalkeepers, a number of soccer balls, 16 cones. The server passes the ball to a wide player who moves down the wing (6.35). The wide player crosses the ball to either the near or far post as the attacking players time their runs in an attempt to head and score.

Goalkeeping
(Handling—Ground and Air Shots)

Organization. Goalkeeper, one player with a number of soccer balls. The goalkeeper stands in the middle of the goal. The server stands at the edge of the penalty area and drives ground and air shots towards the goal (6.36). The goalkeeper should catch each shot using the correct technique.

6.36

Goalkeeping
(Handling—Ground
and Air Shots)

6.37

Organization. Goalkeeper, one player with a number of soccer balls, one cone. The goalkeeper stands in the goal on the goal line. The player stands 10 yards out from the goal with a ball. The goalkeeper sprints forward and touches the cone at the edge of the six-yard box (6.37). As the goalkeeper retreats backwards the player throws the soccer ball high overhead for the goalkeeper to deflect or catch. Repeat the exercise.

Goalkeeping
(Handling, Including Footwork)

Field Size. 40 yds × 40 yds.

Organization. Four-on-four plus a goalkeeper, one soccer ball, seven cones. The cones are set out as goals in a triangular pattern eight yards apart in the middle of the grid. A four-on-four confrontation is played where both teams can score through any of the three goals (6.38). The goalkeeper must scurry between all goals and attempt to keep both teams from scoring. If a save is made, the goalkeeper serves the ball back anywhere within the grid area.

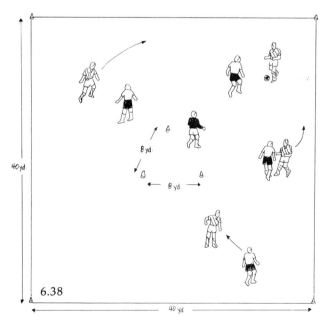

6.38

Goalkeeping
(Shot Stopping)

6.39

Organization. Goalkeeper, one player with a number of soccer balls. The goalkeeper stands in the middle of the goal. The player stands on the six-yard line with the soccer balls and rolls a ball along the ground to the side forcing the goalkeeper to make a low, diving save (6.39). The player fol-

lows by playing another ball high to the opposite side making the goalkeeper dive high to save it. Repeat this exercise ten times remembering to alternate the serving passes, high and low and from side to side.

Goalkeeping
(Shot Stopping)

6.40

Organization. Goalkeeper, one player with a number of soccer balls, eight cones. The goalkeeper stands in the middle of the goal. The player stands 10 to 12 yards from the goal with the soccer balls. The cones are placed across the six-yard line (6.40). The player plays the ball towards the goalkeeper while attempting to hit one of the cones. The cone deflects the ball and forces the goalkeeper to dive to make the save.

Goalkeeping
(Shot Stopping &
Supporting the Defense)

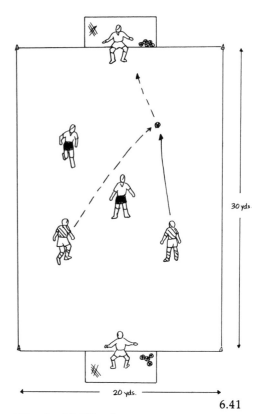

30 yds

20 yds.

6.41

Field Size. 30 yds × 20 yds.

Organization. Two-on-two plus two goalkeepers. Play two-on-two with emphasis on shot stopping, communication, and support of teammates (6.41).

Field Size. Half of the field.

Organization. Goalkeeper, two players with a number of soccer balls. Position the goalkeeper in the goal area. Two players are positioned one on each side of the penalty area. They take turns at crossing the ball to the goalkeeper who catches and throws out to the player on the opposite side of the penalty area (6.42). The player receiving the ball is free to move anywhere down the side of the field. This will encourage the goalkeeper to look and switch play.

6.42

Goalkeeping (Distribution)

6.43

Field Size. Half of the field.

Organization. Goalkeeper, two players, with a number of soccer balls, six cones. The cones are set up 15 yards apart along the center line. The goalkeeper receives a ball from the serving player (6.43). The goalkeeper then distributes it to the other player who calls and is free to move into any one of the three target areas. This will encourage the goalkeeper to look before distributing the ball.

Field Size. Half of the field.

Organization. Goalkeeper, three players with a number of soccer balls. The players on each side of the penalty box take turns at crossing a ball into the goalkeeper to collect in the penalty area (6.44). The goalkeeper can distribute it (kick or throw) back to either of the serving players or to the third player positioned in the center of the field. As the goalkeeper becomes more competent, the coach should nominate which player the goalkeeper should distribute to. This will encourage the goalkeeper in decision-making and quick distribution.

6.44

151

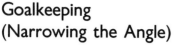

Goalkeeping
(Narrowing the Angle)

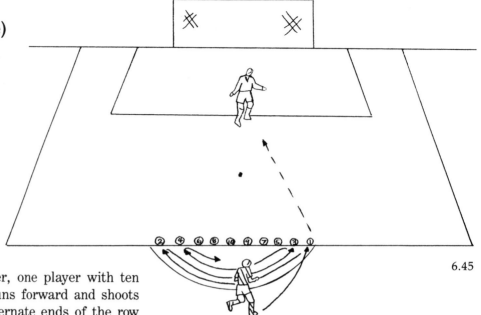

6.45

Organization. Goalkeeper, one player with ten soccer balls. The player runs forward and shoots each ball in turn from alternate ends of the row (6.45). Before each shot the goalkeeper must narrow the angle and attempt to save, then readjust for the next shot.

Goalkeeping
(Narrowing the Angle)

Field Size. 44 yds × 36 yds.

Organization. Twelve players and two goalkeepers with a number of soccer balls. Practice takes place in a double-sized penalty area with full-size goals. To start the practice one of the goalkeepers rolls a ball out to a player on the right side (6.46). The receiving player is chased by another player coming from the opposite side of the goal. The goalkeeper at the far end advances and attempts to narrow the angle and make the save. The receiving goalkeeper should now roll the ball to the right, repeating the exercise. Duplicate this exercise ten times, then change the service to the left.

6.46

152

6.47

Field Size. 40 yds × full field width.

Organization. Four-on-two, plus a goalkeeper and one other player with a number of soccer balls. The serving player passes the ball to any one of the four attacking players. With no offside law and the advantage in numbers, the attacking players should have many opportunities to dribble past or shoot at the goalkeeper (6.47). Once the attackers have broken clear of the defenders, the goalkeeper can practice the skill of narrowing the angle. Encourage the goalkeeper to communicate with the defenders.

Goalkeeping
(Dealing with Crosses)

6.48

Field Size. Half of the field.

Organization. Two players, two goalkeepers, each with a number of soccer balls. One goalkeeper throws a ball to the player on the right who controls and pushes it forward before crossing it to the other goalkeeper (6.48). The receiving goalkeeper collects and repeats the exercise. Duplicate 10 times to the right, then switch to the left to enable the goalkeepers to practice collecting crosses from each side.

153

Goalkeeping (Dealing with Crosses)

6.49

Field Size. Half of the field.

Organization. Three players and one defender, plus a goalkeeper, a number of balls. The serving player passes the ball out to one of the players on the wing. The wing player plays it forward before crossing it into the goal area (6.49). Repeat the exercise passing the ball at varying heights and angles, with the goalkeeper deciding which one should clear the cross.

Goalkeeping (Dealing with Crosses)

Field Size. Half of the field.

Organization. 10 players, two goalkeepers each with a number of soccer balls. One of the goalkeepers throws a ball out to either of the wide players who play it forward before crossing it towards two attacking players in the goal area (6.50). The crosses should be varied between the near and far posts, encouraging the goalkeeper to make decisions and communicate with the defenders. The practice is then repeated from the opposite end.

6.50

154

60 yds.

65 yds.

Field Size.
Half of the field.

Coaching Points

- Spreading the opposition.
- Attacking wide down the wings.
- Switching the point of attack.

6.51

Organization. 10 players plus two goalkeepers, one soccer ball, 16 cones, one portable goal. Set out the half-field with portable goals and smaller cone-indicated goals at the corners on the goal line at each end. Play five-on-five with the exception of corner kicks. Teams get one point for scoring on the goalkeeper and half a point for scoring on the small cone goals (6.51). Always play to a half-point total—e.g., 5½, 6½—to encourage scoring on the small goals.

70 yds

10 yds.

10 yds.

60 yds.

Field Size.
Half of the field.

Organization. Equal teams plus goalkeepers, one soccer ball, 16 cones, one portable goal. Set out the field with the portable goal and 10-yard by 10-yard cone grids at the goal line in each corner. Playing normal soccer each team attempts to free a player into one of the grids (6.52). Once in this grid area, the player should deliver a cross.

6.52

Team Games

6.53

Field Size. 60 yds × 40 yds.

Organization. Team players numbered 1–6, four players without numbers, two goalkeepers, one soccer ball, four cones, one portable goal. Playing six-on-four, once the numbered players have possession of the ball, they must pass it in numerical order (6.53). If the ball is lost, when it is regained passing is recommended in numerical order from the player that has possession. When the players without numbers have possession of the ball they should pass it freely.

Progression. Build up to six-on-five and six-on-six.

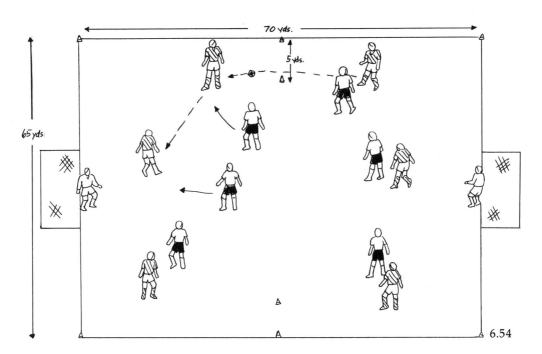

6.54

Field Size. 70 yds × 65 yds.

Organization. Teams with an equal number of players plus goalkeepers, one soccer ball, eight cones. Once a team wins possession of the ball, it must be played through one of the two cone gates before a goal can be scored (6.54). The ball can be thrown in with a correct throw-in, dribbled, or passed through either of the gates from either side.

Field Size. 45 yds × 15 yds.

Organization. Six players, one soccer ball, 12 cones. Set up three 10-yard by 10-yard grids in a triangle, 15 yards by 45 yards. Play three-on-one in one grid, with a single player in the other two grids (6.55). The three players complete a series of passes then chip the ball to a player in one of the other two grids. The three players sprint to that grid; the last player to arrive becomes the defender, and the exercise is repeated. To keep the runners from cheating, the defender performs 20 push-ups after the attackers leave the grid.

Progression. Change the point of attack; play four-on-two and increase up to five grids.

6.55

Coaching Points

- Sprint to support players quickly.
- Accuracy of the chip.
- Get passes in quickly.
- Game related—switching the point of attack and providing quick support.

Coaching Points

- Work on team transition
- Attacking
- Defending

6.56

Field Size. Half of the field.

Organization. 12 players plus two goalkeepers, one soccer ball. The goalkeepers are the *target* and are restricted, one to the six-yard box and the other to half of the center circle (6.56). The teams attempt to play the ball to a *target*. If the ball is delivered from a *wide position,* a *lofted pass* must be used. If the ball is delivered from a *central position* a *ground shot* must be used. As soon as a team reaches the *target* the ball is distributed back to that same team, which then attacks in the opposite direction.

157

ABOUT THE AUTHORS

Robert "Butch" Lauffer

Robert "Butch" Lauffer has been playing soccer since the age of seven, and today is one of a new generation of young soccer coaches who grew up playing the game of soccer in the United States and abroad.

Until recently Mr. Lauffer was Coaching Director of the Spring Soccer Club, in Spring, Texas, which has a youth enrollment of over one thousand players. Presently Mr. Lauffer is the Men's Head Soccer Coach at West Texas State University in Canyon, Texas.

He progressed to the North Texas Soccer Association under-19 state team in 1979 and 1980. Butch went on to play with the famed Texas Longhorns Soccer Club in Dallas. He played in over 100 international games for the club, travelling to Mexico, England, Scotland, Wales, Finland, West Germany, Austria, Norway, Luxemburg, Italy, France, Sweden, and Denmark, in addition to tournaments such as the Gothia Cup (twice), the Helsinki Cup, and the Munich Cup. The Longhorns' 1980 win of the Munich Cup was a tremendous upset, as this was the first United States team to win a major European tournament. Later he coached and travelled with the Texas Longhorns' under-12, under-14, and under-16 teams to England and Scotland—all by the age of 20.

Mr. Lauffer attended the Carnegie School of Physical Education and Human Movement in Leeds, England, from 1981 to 1983, where he played soccer and earned Player of the Year honors in 1983. He returned to the United States and received a Bachelor of Science Degree in Kinesiology from Texas Christian University, where he was also captain of the soccer team. He also received his Master's Degree from T.C.U. in 1988 after serving as the Graduate Assistant Coach to both Men's and Women's Division I Soccer.

From 1984 to 1986, Butch worked with the North Texas Soccer Association, and presently with the South Texas Soccer Association, in the training and selection of players for the State Team, as well as conducting licensing courses for coaches. He was Staff Coach for the United States Youth Soccer Association in 1987 for Region 3, and a National Team Administrator for the United States Soccer Federation Under-16 tour of Scotland in 1988, and the under-20 trip to the Interregional Tournament in Las Cruces, N.M., in 1988 and their trip to the Granatkin Tournament in Russia in 1989.

His coaching education includes the United States Soccer Federation "A" License, the Irish Football Association Full Badge, the N.S.C.A.A. Advanced National Diploma, The English Football Association Preparatory Course and Preliminary Badge. He is also the author of *Coaching Soccer*.

Alexander "Sandy" Davie

Sandy is a United States Soccer Federation "A" licensed coach and also holds New Zealand's highest F.I.F.A. coaching qualification, the Advanced-Level Senior Coaching Certificate. Having played in 27 countries, Sandy is both an internationally accomplished player as well as a coach. His coaching abilities stem from a professional playing career which began at age 15. Sandy now brings his wealth of knowledge and experience to the Southwest Florida region where he is currently the Soccer Coaching Consultant for the City of Fort Myers, which serves the Lee County School District through the Stars (Success through academic and recreational support) Program. He also conducts and assists at coaching clinics throughout the country.

Sandy's distinguished career in soccer commenced when he was signed at age 15 by Dundee United, a Scottish First Division Club, as their Goalkeeper. During his seven years with Dundee United, he played over 200 games including European competition against Barcelona of Spain and Juventus of Italy. In 1961 Sandy was selected twice for the Scottish Youth International Team against Wales and England. From 1964 to 1966 he represented the under 23 Scottish Team four times, twice against England, and one time each against Wales and France. Following a transfer in 1967 to Luton Town F.C. of the English Third Division, Sandy assisted in promoting the club to the Second Division in 1969, playing over 100 first-team games with them. Later that year Sandy graced Southampton, F.C. of the English First Division with his abilities, and was a member of the team which played in the European Union of Football Associations Cup competition against Atletico Bilbao of Spain. In 1971, Sandy returned to his hometown team, Dundee United F.C., and in 1974, played in the team's first-ever appearance in the Scottish Cup Final at Hampden Park against Glasgow Celtic before a crowd of 98,000.

Following the Scottish Cup Final he emigrated to New Zealand and played for the North Shore Club in Auckland. He became player/coach in 1976 and assisted the club in winning the 1977 National Championship before transferring to another Auckland Club, Mount Wellington A.F.C. later that year. In 1979 Mount Wellington became the National League Champions and Sandy was chosen as the Auckland "Sportsman of the Year." The team went on to win National League and Cup doubles in 1980 and 1982.

During the years 1978 to 1982 Sandy represented New Zealand 32 times in full International matches. He qualified as a Senior Coach with the New Zealand Soccer Association in 1981 and was the New Zealand Soccer Association's Liaison Officer to the Chinese Taipei World Cup Soccer Squad during the 1982 World Cup Preliminary Rounds. Sandy turned his talents towards an ever increas-ing coaching commitment, compiled articles for national newspapers and sporting publications, while furthering his international experience as a tour guide for the New Zealand Government Tourist Bureau to the 1982 World Cup in Spain. He was also utilized by New Zealand national television and radio for commentary work, and in the area of raising funds for charity organizations. From 1983 until 1986 Sandy was the Director of Coaching for the Auckland Women's Soccer Association and Technical Director of a Super Skills Program that he and the Administrative Director compiled and implemented for the New Zealand Soccer Association.

He became National Goalkeeper Coach for the New Zealand Soccer Association and was also the New Zealand Women's National Team Coach from 1984 to 1986. During this time the Women's Team finished second in the Oceania Tournament two times and achieved a Federation de Football Association world ranking of fourth at the Women's World Invitational Tournament in Taiwan.

In 1987 Sandy moved to Australia where once again his coaching abilities were put to good use by the Queensland Soccer Coaches Association. In the summer of 1989 while Sandy was a Staff Coach at Duke University's Summer Soccer Camp in North Carolina, he was offered the position of Assistant Director of Coaching for the Lone Stars, the competitive program of the Spring Soccer Club, Inc. of Houston, Texas. During 1990 his experience was utilized at summer camps held at Canterbury Soccer Club, Atlanta, Ga., U.N.C. Wilmington, N.C., and once again at Duke University where he was approached for his current appointment.

INDEX

Abdomen, lower, for aerial control, 34 *illus.*
Aerial control, 146–147 *illus.*
  chest, 34–35 *illus.*
  inside of foot, 32 *illus.*
  instep, 33 *illus.*
  lower abdomen, 34 *illus.*
  practice
    for under age 8, 58–60 *illus.*
    for under age 10, 83–84 *illus.*
    for under age 12, 116–119 *illus.*
  thigh, 33 *illus.*
Attacking
  half volley, 26 *illus.*
  heading and, 37, 119 *illus.*
  inside of foot volley—across the line, 24 *illus.*
  instep volley, 20–21 *illus.*
  instep volley—across the line, 24–25 *illus.*
  outside of foot volley, 21–23 *illus.*
  principles of, 66 *illus.*
Attacking third of field, dribbling and, 8

Calves stretch, 44 *illus.*
Chest, for aerial control, 34–35 *illus.*
Chipping, 19 *illus.*
Coaches, needs of, 5
Control
  aerial. *See* Aerial control
  ground. *See* Ground control
  lofted passing, 115 *illus.*
  passing, 138 *illus.*, 141–145 *illus.*
  principles of, 27
Crossing, 113–114 *illus.*

Dead ball, distribution, kicking, 63 *illus.*
Defending
  heading and, 37, 120 *illus.*
  inside of foot and instep volleys— across the line, 25 *illus.*
  inside of foot volley, 23 *illus.*
Defense, principles of, 66 *illus.*
Distribution
  goalkeeping, 125–126 *illus.*, 151 *illus.*
  goal kick, 124 *illus.*
  javelin throw, 91 *illus.*
  kicking—dead ball, 63 *illus.*
  kicking—half volley, 64 *illus.*
  kicking—volley, 63 *illus.*
  underarm throw, 91 *illus.*
Diving, by goalkeeper, 42 *illus.*
Dribbling, 7–8 *illus.*
  effective, qualities of, 9
  practice
    for under age 8, 49–50 *illus.*
    for under age 12, 105–107 *illus.*
    for under age 15, 134–135 *illus.*

Feints, 9
Five-on-one, 99 *illus.*
Five-on-two, 100 *illus.*

Flesh wounds, 45
Fluids, 45
Foot, surfaces for dribbling, 8
Full volleys, 20–26 *illus.*

Goalkeeping, 39
  basic handling practice, 121–122 *illus.*
  chest shots, handling, 90 *illus.*
  crosses—catching, 127–128 *illus.*
  dealing with crosses, 153 *illus.*
  distribution, 125–126 *illus.*, 151 *illus.*
    goal kick, 124 *illus.*
    javelin throw, 91 *illus.*
    kicking—dead ball, 63 *illus.*
    kicking—half volley, 64 *illus.*
    kicking—volley, 63 *illus.*
    underarm throw, 91 *illus.*
  diving, 42 *illus.*
  ground and air shots, handling, 149 *illus.*
  ground shots, handling of, 40 *illus.*
  handling including footwork, 149 *illus.*
  head-high shots and above, handling of, 41 *illus.*
  narrowing the angle, 128–129 *illus.*, 152–153 *illus.*
  overarm throw, 92 *illus.*
  practice
    for under age 8, 62–65 *illus.*
    for under age 10, 88–93 *illus.*
  punching, 128 *illus.*
  shot stopping, 55 *illus.*, 92–93 *illus.*, 122–123 *illus.*, 150 *illus.*
  shot stopping and supporting the defense, 150 *illus.*
  starting position, 39 *illus.*
  waist-chest shots, handling, 90 *illus.*
  waist high shots, handling of, 41 *illus.*
Ground control, 115 *illus.*
  inside of foot, 28 *illus.*
  outside of foot, 28–29 *illus.*
  practice
    for under age 8, 57–58 *illus.*
    for under age 10, 81–82 *illus.*
  sole of foot, 32 *illus.*
  and turning—inside of foot, 29–30 *illus.*
  and turning—outside of foot, 31 *illus.*
Ground kneeling technique, for goalkeeping, 40 *illus.*, 88–89 *illus.*

Hamstrings stretch, 44 *illus.*
Heading
  attacking practice, for under age 12, 119 *illus.*
  defending, 120 *illus.*
  feet on the ground, 36–37 *illus.*
  feet off the ground, 37
  one-footed takeoff, 37
  practice
    for under age 8, 60–61 *illus.*
    for under age 10, 84–85 *illus.*
  practices for under age 15, 148 *illus.*
  two-footed takeoff, 38 *illus.*
Heat cramps, 45
Heat exhaustion, 45
Heat stroke, 45

Injury management, 42–46
Instep drive, 16 *illus.*, 55–56 *illus.*
Instep kicking, 75–76 *illus.*

Keep away, 131 *illus.*
Kicking
  inside of foot, 108–110 *illus.*
  with inside of foot, 74–75 *illus.*
  with outside of foot, 17 *illus.*, 77–79 *illus.*
Kicking—shooting practice, 136–137 *illus.*
Kicking—volleys, 111 *illus.*, 137–137 *illus.*
Kicking—volleys—shooting, 111 *illus.*
Kneeling technique, for goalkeeping, 40 *illus.*, 88–89 *illus.*

Lofted pass, 18 *illus.*, 112–115 *illus.*, 141 *illus.*

Passing, 12–15 *illus.*, 138 *illus.*
  control, 141–145 *illus.*
  inside of foot, 51–53 *illus.*, 108–110 *illus.*
  inside the foot, 146 *illus.*
  lofted, 18 *illus.*, 112–115 *illus.*, 141 *illus.*
  outside of foot, 53–54 *illus.*
  practice, for under age 8, 51–54 *illus.*
Passing—crosses practice, 139–140 *illus.*
Player's performance, 2
Push pass, 13–14 *illus.*

Shielding, 10–12 *illus.*, 70–71 *illus.*, 105–106 *illus.*
Shin splints, 45
Shot stopping, for goalkeeping, 122–123 *illus.*
Sideways—on approach to ball, 30 *illus.*
Splints, 46
Stoop technique, for goalkeeping, 40 *illus.*, 62–63 *illus.*
Striking at the goal, inside of foot volley, 20 *illus.*
Swerve pass, 14–15 *illus.*

Tackling, 36 *illus.*, 86–87 *illus.*
Team formation, for under age 10, 101–102 *illus.*
Team games
  for under age 8, 67–68 *illus.*
  for under age 10, 94–95 *illus.*
  for under age 12, 130–131 *illus.*
  for under age 15, 156–157 *illus.*
Teams, getting to spread out, 96–100 *illus.*
Thigh, for aerial control, 33 *illus.*
Three-on-one, 97 *illus.*
Three-on-two, 98 *illus.*
Three-on-zero, 96 *illus.*

Warm-up
  for under age 8, 48 *illus.*
  for under age 10, 70 *illus.*
  for under age 12, 104–105 *illus.*
  for under age 15, 133 *illus.*